GOING IT ALONE

GOING IT ALONE

RAMBLINGS AND REFLECTIONS
FROM THE TRAIL

∎ ∎ ∎

TIM HAUSERMAN

UNIVERSITY OF NEVADA PRESS | *Reno & Las Vegas*

University of Nevada Press | Reno, Nevada 89557 USA
www.unpress.nevada.edu
Copyright © 2022 by University of Nevada Press
All rights reserved
Cover photographs © iStock/Paigefalk

LIBRARY OF CONGRESS CATALOGING-IN-PUBLICATION DATA
Names: Hauserman, Tim, 1958– author.
Title: Going it alone : ramblings and reflections from the trail / Tim Hauserman.
Description: Reno ; Las Vegas : University of Nevada Press, [2022] |
Summary: "*Solo* is the story of the conflict between the joy and loneliness Tim
    Hauserman discovered on a series of backpack trips in the wilderness: a tale
    of self-induced misadventures and overwhelming sadness but also many
    moments of sublime rapture. It is a humorous, humble take on the experience
    of spending time alone in the wilderness—part exquisite nature journal, part
    Bill Bryson in the woods—with a unique voice and take on the world."—
    Provided by publisher.
Identifiers: LCCN 2022003336 | ISBN 9781647790653 (paperback) |
    ISBN 9781647790660 (ebook)
Subjects: LCSH: Hauserman, Tim, 1958—Anecdotes. | Backpacking—Anecdotes. |
    Loneliness. | Solitude.
Classification: LCC GV199.6 .H3794 2022 | DDC 796.51—dc23/eng/20220201
LC record available at https://lccn.loc.gov/2022003336

The paper used in this book meets the requirements of American National
Standard for Information Sciences—Permanence of Paper for Printed Library
Materials, ANSI/NISO Z39.48-1992 (R2002).

FIRST PRINTING

Manufactured in the United States of America

For the trail builders.
Thanks for creating little ribbons across the land
that allow me to face challenges
and find peace.

Contents

Illustrations follow pages 40 and 102

Acknowledgments

It's ironic that the COVID-19 pandemic is the first thing that comes to my mind when thinking about whom, or in this case, what, to thank for the completion of this book. Sure, COVID-19 has been devastating and frustrating and draining, but when freelance writing and life in general took a break in March 2020, I was finally forced to revisit a draft of this book. It had been languishing for years just waiting for me to be stuck with nothing else to do. I now had no distractions or excuses.

The pandemic encouraged my writing friend Lisa Michelle to form the Cabin Fever Writers, a group of writers who were too far apart to get together in person, so the Zoom meetings of the pandemic made it happen. We met virtually almost every week for about six months to critique each other's work. Sure, the suggestions sometimes seemed brutal—none of us like to kill our darlings—but they made for better books. Lisa's thriller *Blue Mountain,* published in September 2021, was a product of the group, as is a stunning memoir by Bridey Heidel that's soon to be published.

While the focus of this book is my solo hiking, I was still part of a community of hikers who joined me on other hikes or who acted as trail angels. Special kudos to Jan Corda, Joe Pace, and my cousin, Cindi Little, who went above and beyond. And of course, all those backpacking trips with my daughters, Sarah and Hannah, were also an impetus to keep me hiking.

Two anonymous reviewers with the University of Nevada Press made a number of suggestions that dramatically improved the book, and editor Paul Szydelko put every sentence through a fine-toothed comb to make it as good as possible.

Finally, I'd like to thank Joyce Chambers, who reads all my stuff, gently gives me advice, and is always up for a hike…well, almost always, as long as it isn't too cold.

GOING IT ALONE

What Was I Thinking?

AFTER DECADES of day hiking by myself, I decided I no longer wanted to go home at night. I wanted to feel the air slowly chill while watching the sun drop behind the stark peaks of the Sierra Nevada. Lie on stone in the wilderness as the countless stars begin to appear in the absolute darkness. Catch the sun fire up the granite peaks as the morning rays slowly warm my tent. And experience it all solo, with the only sounds being wind rustling through pine needles, birds flitting through trees, and the soft crunch of my feet on dirt.

This is the story of what I discovered by setting out on my own into the wilderness. I found moments of utter joy and peace but also sheer, gut-wrenching loneliness. I faced a continual battle between the forces in my brain that cried out for companionship and the part of me that was elated by the power of nature's grandeur to light up my solo soul.

Loneliness is something we try not to talk about. Men especially consider it a sign of weakness, something that just needs to be bucked up and got on with. Yet, like many of the things that we refuse to talk about, it's an important and universal commonality of life. Sorta like death and masturbation. Everyone faces loneliness. To fight it off, we surround ourselves with friends, conversations, screens, whatever kinds of noise we can to keep us from facing our inner quiet. We go to bars, restaurants, school, online, or anywhere we might be able to talk and relate and communicate with other humans. Some even find or stay in bad relationships, just so they have a person to talk to, or not talk to, but at least be pissed off at, which also helps keep the mind occupied so it doesn't have time to think about being lonely.

In his essay "Fear of Rest," Wayne Muller writes:

Our unspoken fears and sadnesses speed up our lives. We are terrified of the painful grief that is hot to touch, sharp and piercing, so we keep moving, faster, and faster, so we will not feel how sad we are, how much we have lost in this life: strength, youthful playfulness, so many friends and lovers, dreams that did not come true, all that have passed away. When we stop even for a moment, we can feel the burning, empty hole in our belly. So we keep moving, afraid the empty fire of loss will consume us....

While our speed may keep us safe, it also keeps us malnourished. It prevents us from tasting those things that would truly make us safe. Prayer, touch, kindness, fragrance—all those things that live in rest, and not in speed.

It is when I escape from civilization and head out alone into the woods that I can hear what is really going on inside my head. Sometimes nature brings bliss and a cleansing healing. It fills my soul with gratitude to be given the gift of time spent in the wilderness. But sometimes joy and peace are replaced by fear, angst, and a hollow space filled with twirling butterflies. Sometimes I am John Muir, the conservationist. Sometimes Woody Allen (obviously the neurotic *Annie Hall* version, not the real-life one).

In his essay, Muller said: "Emptiness is the pregnant void out of which all creation springs. But many of us fear emptiness.... It feels like an abyss, a sheer drop into eternity, a dangerous negation of all that is alive, visible, safe and good."

When I set out alone into the wilderness, my goal was simple: to spend more time experiencing the beauty of the natural world right outside my door. I quickly realized that nature's beauty was just the enticement that brought me to the true benefits of spending a lengthy chunk of time alone. The silent time, away from people and screens, gave my brain the chance to slow down and escape the veneer of life in the civilized world. At times, this brought me the relaxed calm and even profound joy for which I was searching.

But these trips also enrolled me in a very challenging course that will take a lifetime to complete. Initially, I thought the title for this school of hard knocks should be "How to Conquer All this Damn Loneliness." But then after a lot of failed exams, I finally came to realize it's not about eliminating the emptiness but learning how to sit in the core of the hollow and find peace there.

It's about understanding the difference between solitude and loneliness. Hara Estroff Marano wrote in *Psychology Today*:

Loneliness is a negative state, marked by a sense of isolation. One feels that something is missing. It is possible to be with people and still feel lonely—perhaps the most bitter form of loneliness. Solitude is the state of being alone without being lonely. It is a positive and constructive state of engagement with oneself. Solitude is desirable, a state of being alone where you provide yourself wonderful and sufficient company.

This sounds wonderful, and in my mind when I go tromping off into the woods, I'm the cheerful eighth member of Snow White's dwarf troop whistling down the trail. I'm sure I can invoke my inner Muir, who said, "To sit in solitude, to think in solitude with only the music of the stream and the cedar to break the flow of silence, there lies the value of wilderness." I do look at nature and feel that joy of solitude most of the time. But then, "Geez, Louise," out pops the dark lord inside my brain who starts reminding me in the night that if something bad happens right now, I'm in deep doo-doo.

■ ■ ■

Every day, I stare at a computer and attempt the arduous process of rassling words out of the deep cobwebby recesses of my brain. Somehow those words must travel through millions of miles of questionable brain matter through my fingers to the screen. There are lots of places along this journey for the right word to take a wrong turn and head off after a squirrel, in which case the word, like a bubble, pops and disappears. Fortunately, like most writers, I've discovered valuable tools to deal with the frustration that comes from attempting to bring those words to the screen. Notice I said I have tools to deal with the frustration, not actually assist with the word retrieval. That's magic, and nobody really knows how in the hell it works; we just want to be there with our fingers poised to plink when it does.

My primary method of dealing with the challenges of writing is procrastination and avoidance. For many years, a day on a bike rolling through the forest, or a hike to the shore of a mountain lake, has been my favorite form of avoidance, bringing me relaxation and bliss and a chance for my brain to recalibrate from all that word wrangling. This diversion also fits in well with my primary addiction: exercise. If I go a day or two without a few hours of huffing and puffing, I start climbing walls. A few more days, and I start twitching and snapping at folks for having the audacity to say hello.

* * *

Growing up, I didn't do a lot of backpacking. But about twenty years ago, I added it to my repertoire of escape techniques. I discovered that if everything you need is on your back, everywhere you go is home. And while the accommodations in the woods are a bit rustic, the views are sublime. You get to watch the sun quietly fall behind the ridgeline and usher in the calm stillness of evening and, next morning, witness the sun slowly march its way down to your home.

After several backpacking trips with friends, I decided to embark on my first solo trip. I'd spent a lot of time hiking alone and always appreciated that quiet time for reflection and connection. I didn't understand that it was actually a giant leap from hiking alone during the day to spending a number of days in the wilderness.

1

Howling at the Half Moon

S THE SUN WANED, I sat on the shore of the aptly named Half Moon Lake, tucked at the end of a deep cirque surrounded by three massive peaks in the heart of the Desolation Wilderness just west of Lake Tahoe. Steeply rising volcanic slopes covered in brush reach 2,000 feet higher from the shore of the lake to the rocky summits of Dicks and Jacks Peaks. When the gentle breeze momentarily waned, the distant sound of a waterfall wafted to my campsite, then disappeared with the next gust of wind. It was my first trip into the wilderness alone, and I was the only human in this place of profound tranquility. But when darkness fell, my stomach churned, a deep pit of loneliness. It was like the incapacitating dizziness I get while peering over the edge of a cliff.

A battle raged within my head and spine. The Woody Allen side, which usually only comes out at night, is dominated by fear, and the possibility that if anything can go wrong, it just might. The John Muir side, however, was happily marveling at the shimmering water and the craggy bark of the juniper trees and was perfectly comfortable with the situation. The Muir muse tried to convince me that when I looked back at this trip, I would only remember the beauty of nature, not the moments of loneliness. But as I felt fear along the shore of the lake, I was reminded that while the hike was temporary, the conditions that led me to be there by myself were not.

I was married, but we were two solos living together, each focusing on our own approaches to life. We were great at being parents and friends but weak at finding things to do as a couple. She had no interest in hiking or backpacking. And I had no interest in not hiking and backpacking.

While I would venture out onto trips by myself, every year I'd also take two short backpack trips with my daughters, which began when they were six and eight years old. It was a chance to fully focus on one daughter at a time away from the distractions of their lives, and it was one of the most important experiences I had with them during their childhoods. Although their eyes would roll when I would point and exclaim, "That's a lodgepole pine!" or, "Wow, look at that lake," I still believe it was a memorable part of their young lives. As they moved into their teen years, however, they became less interested in setting out into the woods with Dad. They were busy practicing their pirouettes or studying for the SATs.

Hannah, the younger, bowed out first at 14. One of her last trips was a joint trip with my older daughter Sarah and me to Paradise Lake, near Donner Summit. It truly lived up to its name in the middle of the summer: cool, clear water and, just offshore, granite, whale-shaped islands, luring us into the water. At seven miles to the lake, it was way past Hannah's comfort zone for a hike, but the promised, blissful layover day spurred her on to a dog-tired completion. Ah, the layover day, a chance to spend the day doing nothing but flying off rocky precipices into the crisp, deep water below, followed by a few frantic strokes to the island refuges, where resting on the warm rocks eased the chill until it was time to head to shore for lunch.

Sarah kept backpacking for a few more years, and with such fond memories of that layover day at Paradise Lake, I was able to entice her into going back for another piece of paradise. This trip, however, was more like hell.

Sarah brought a trusted friend and her accompanying dad. As we hiked to the lake on a beautiful, blue-sky August day, our minds were full of visions of our last layover day in Paradise, how we had spent the whole day relaxing on the lakeshore. Yeah, we shoulda done that on this trip. Instead, on our layover day, we made the easy jaunt to the other side of the lake and gazed down at neighboring Warren Lake, which set deep in a bowl at the bottom of a precipitous drop far below. Unfortunately, we were focused on the allure of the shimmering water of the lake and not the challenge of getting there, and more importantly, back. But I was not very skilled at passing up the chance to take on the challenge of exploring a beautiful lake.

Because there were no direct trails between Paradise and Warren Lakes, we bushwhacked down the precariously steep terrain and crawled through thick, scratchy brush, while praying that we wouldn't tumble down one of the sheer embankments that we gingerly slid down. Finally, disheveled, distraught, and covered in bloody scratches, we made it to the lake.

Looking back at what we had just done, we realized that attempting to go back up the route we had come down would be even harder. Being a dad, I made the executive decision that it wouldn't be safe to try, so we took the much longer way back via the Warren Lake Trail.

The description of the Warren Lake Trail in the guidebook *Tahoe Sierra* reads: "From this you'll drop 1000 feet on one of the steepest knee-jarring trails imaginable. Constrained by encroaching bedrock, the trail tries vainly to ease the grade with dozens of minuscule switchbacks.... You'll need a well earned layover day at Warren Lake."

It's probably a good thing nineteen-year-old Sarah didn't read that description, since we did it in the opposite direction. After climbing dozens of steep, grueling switchbacks, she stopped in tears and said, "I'm not going to make it.... I'm going to die!" She didn't really have a flair for the dramatic, so I was concerned, but there were no other options but to keep hiking. I'm sure she appreciated my suggestion that we should step it up a bit so we wouldn't run out of daylight.

Once we crested the saddle, we still had a lengthy bushwhack up a steep ridgeline to the top of 9,000-foot-plus Basin Peak, followed by a long slog on a dusty trail back to Paradise Lake. We finally reached the lake as the sun was starting to drop below the peaks. Long before we stumbled into camp, Sarah and her friend had stopped talking to me. I thought I heard them spit out something about "ten miles of climbing; this is not a layover day." They were right. They had messed up. They had trusted me. We had failed the first law of layover days. And Sarah hasn't backpacked with me since.

■ ■ ■

A cabal of three females surrounded me at home now. They stayed inside and did crafts (to me, the word "crafts" grates like fingernails on a chalkboard), while I shoveled the snow off the back deck; watched *Gilmore Girls,* while I made the French toast; and stayed home in their jammies, while I began venturing out solo on longer explorations into the wilderness.

2

What the Q?

THE SMOOTH ROCK LED GENTLY to the shore of one of the little lakes known as the 4-Qs. Bonsai trees sprouted out of mini granite islands as gnarled whitebark pines held fast to cracks in the rocks just above the gentle lapping of waves. Meanwhile, I reclined on the granite, making a valiant effort to keep lonely thoughts from fluttering around in my head, but that pit in my stomach was even more cavernous on this trip than on the last one.

I attempted to distract myself with the dream that these lakes were named the Qs because the cartographer couldn't figure out what to call four teensy dots of water, so she just put a Q on top of them, as in, "Question: what the hell are these?"

The 4-Qs are in a remote western edge of the not-very-remote Desolation Wilderness, at the end of a dwindling excuse for a hiking trail, which begins next to the leaning remains of an ancient wooden sign that says, "Trail is not maintained and is not recommended." They might as well have just put up a skull and crossbones.

■ ■ ■

A year after my trip to Half Moon Lake, I hiked into the Qs in early October, which meant that the days were short and not a lot of light was available for nature study. A ton of time, however, permitted an extended session of in-the-dark "navel pondering." That would be thirteen freaking dark hours in a tiny, one-person tent that barely fit a sleeping bag. If you sat up, your head touched the ceiling. That's way more time than I should be allowed to spend alone contemplating my place in the scheme of the universe.

There I was, just above the shore of Question Mark No. 3, thinking these healthy thoughts: this late in the season, located where I was, way off the main parade routes of Desolation, on some trail that people were warned to avoid, if something were to happen to me, it would be at least the following summer before someone would find my desiccated body, lying next to the remains of what the animals left of my tent. The only thing scarier than that prospect is the length of that last sentence.

Given my past experience, it was not much of a stretch imagining something happening to me. It's not that I am always pushing the envelope or a great risk-taker. In fact, I consider myself to be a bit of a chickenshit. It's just that I have always been the guy who is more motivated to take action than skilled at completing said action. In other words, my eyes are bigger than my abilities. Or perhaps I'm just unfairly comparing myself to all those Red Bull–fueled extreme athletes who conquer sheer peaks or hike thousands of miles, while I look at their accomplishments and say, "Well, I should be able to do that."

When I was fifteen years old, I fell off the front of a boat, which was a problem since it was going thirty miles an hour at the time. I arrived in the water quickly, but then time went into slow motion. The muted blue light of the sky shimmered through Tahoe's clear waters, then a dark shadow briefly blocked the sun, followed by bubbles, lots of bubbles, like I was inside a glass of champagne. Then I was bobbing on the surface, watching the boat roar away. My first thought: did they notice I was gone, or would I float for hours treading water, before eventually giving up and sinking into the deep? My second thought: "Hey, look at my left leg!" It was floating on the surface at a cockeyed angle that should not be attempted by anyone who is not a gymnast or that super-limber woman in yoga class, you know the one, who can contort her body like a pretzel and still keep a smile on her face.

Soon, my heroes returned, gingerly plucked me out of the water, and laid me down into the boat. As they rushed me to the beach in Tahoe City, I heard, "Don't let him see his leg!" I mumbled back, "I already did."

It took longer than it normally would to reach the shore, because my knee had bent the propeller. I spent the next two weeks lying in a hospital bed in a cast listening to a string of visitors tell me how lucky I was that the propeller had only hit my leg and not my head. They were right. As I fell headfirst and backward, my legs stayed closer to the surface as the boat roared by while my noggin was safely out of prop range. But all that logic is tough for a teenager to handle—I would have preferred the kind of luck that involved not falling off the damn boat in the first place.

.   .   .

Stupid Tim Trick: A few years after this incident, I heard a story on a local radio station about a woman who had fallen off a boat into Lake Tahoe and her knee had been cut by the propeller. Sensing that I had finally found a field in which I was an expert, I called the hospital to cheer her up. For several minutes, I passed on all kinds of encouraging information about her future before saying, "Hey, I can hike fifteen miles in a day now. In no time you will be up and out there hiking just like me!" There was a lengthy pause on the other end of the line, and then she said, "Oh…you still have your leg?"

.   .   .

When I was eighteen and my brother twenty-one, we were traveling around Europe unsupervised for two months. Near the end of the trip we arrived in Amsterdam, the land of Heineken, legal pot, and red-light districts. The Van Goghs were especially intriguing when the edibles hit, and it looked like the paint was sticking out from the canvas several inches. On the second night, I made an accidental, drunken foray into one of the city's famous canals. I'm still not really sure how I got in, but the water was dirty and slimy, and it smelled like I was inside a subway vent. A sheer stone wall, which rose ten feet from the dark water, separated me from dry land. It was covered in green, slippery goop, meaning there was no easy way out. I sobered up pretty damn fast. It was looking like my story would end at eighteen.

Fortunately, I must have made a loud splash as I stumbled in, because just as I was pondering my bad decisions while treading water, I heard, "Someone fell in!" Soon, some good Samaritans hauled me out of the goo. They removed all my clothes except my underwear to keep me from leaving a trail of green slime on their car seat. My hotel sat on a pedestrian-only street, so my rescuers had to drop me off several hundred yards away from the hotel. With sticky, matted hair, smelling like a sewer, and wearing nothing but slimy underwear, I strolled past a healthy herd of hearty partiers. Even in wild Amsterdam, someone must have said, "Wait, did you see what I just saw?"

There is one more instance when I cheated death. Although I have no recollection of it, one of my lifesavers remembers it well and recently provided me with the details. When I was about six, I was visiting this friend who lived in the Gatekeepers Cabin at the confluence of Lake Tahoe and the Truckee River. Apparently, I managed to get the rope used to access his prized tree house around my neck and then fell through the entrance toward the ground…thereby hanging myself. Fortunately, one of my friends rushed to hold up my feet, while the other wrested the rope off my neck. "We thought you were a goner," my friend concluded his vivid recollection of the event fifty years later. Realizing her son had to save my life and fearing the next time that Hauserman kid might not be so lucky, his mother made him take down the tree house the next day. While I was not a goner, his tree house was.

■ ■ ■

On my backpacking adventures, I've never been seriously injured or forced to chop off a hand or some other limb while trapped between rocks (though if that means reaping the rewards of a best-selling book and acclaimed movie, the writer in me might consider the option). But I have always had enough little things happen (amazing how you can delude yourself into thinking "doing stupid things" is equivalent to "little things happen") to add a certain amount of plausibility to the fears of desiccation I was experiencing at the 4-Qs.

For example, on that first trip at Half Moon Lake, I couldn't get my damn stove to work. As visions of cold food danced in my head, I fiddled with that sucker for a half hour before finally realizing that I had put it together bass-ackward. The next night, having made the long trek past Lake Aloha, over Mosquito Pass, before heading back to Middle Velma Lake, things got interesting. Fortunately, I was lucky enough to have the lake to myself, if only so I wouldn't be embarrassed. I wrote this in my journal:

> I discovered that this great campsite was not as special as it first appeared. It was, in fact, the home of the most obnoxious, determined family of golden-mantled ground squirrels to be found anywhere on the planet. To the unknowing, they may look innocent, happily scampering around like they were the lead characters in an *Alvin* movie, but they are much more sinister and troublesome than bears, mountain lions, or snakes. If I turned around for one second, they were in my pack, sucking on my

CamelBak or furtively gnawing through a bag to pilfer my trail mix. While I valiantly attempted to boil water for dinner, I fought them off with rocks, threw up my arms, and ran after the little bastards, yelling, "Arrrrrr!!!" It's a good thing I was the only person at the lake.

Finally, the water boiled, and I carefully poured the precious fluid into my last remaining dinner pouch, stirred the contents, catching a savory whiff of melting cheese, and delicately put the package down on a rock. I salivated at the prospect of a warm meal, keeping close guard on the packet while I waited the interminable fifteen minutes for it to cook. If you want to slow down time, get very hungry, then wait for a meal to become edible on a backpack trip. After about ten minutes, I couldn't resist chucking just one more rock at one more marauding squirrel that had just leapt onto my pack when it happened. As I lifted up my arm to throw, I lightly grazed my dinner, and then in slow motion, with my mind pumping out accompanying music, it fell to the ground.

Remember the tire-changing scene in *A Christmas Story?* When Ralphie's one-and-only important assignment was to hold on to those pesky bolts needed to change that tire, but instead they went flying into the air, followed shortly thereafter by his illegal use of an F bomb that gets his mouth washed out with soap? Yeah, it was like that. There was an emphatic splat, followed by the contents slowly oozing out onto the dirt, slurping out a gooey mess of muddy, formerly food-like product. After my own F bombs flew, I realized it was getting dark, I was hungry, driven slightly mad by squirrels, and was sure a bear a mile away just lifted up his nose and said, "Hmmm…beef stroganoff with noodles. Oh, I love that one!"

A few minutes later, I was frantically digging a deep hole in the rocky soil with my pooper-scooper, then plopping the goop into the hole. I covered it up with dirt and a few rocks in a feeble attempt to disguise my folly. I returned to my campsite, where I brooded over some important questions: Was it buried deep enough? Was it far enough away from my campsite? Would the animals still find it? And after the bear found it and wolfed it down in a second, would that just whet its appetite for the main course, which "Yogi" would surely believe must be in that tent right over there?

There was little time to ponder, however, as the wind began to blow ferociously across Middle Velma Lake. Waves lapped against the rocky shore; high above, the tree branches tossed back and forth violently in the gale, creating the sound of two dozen dissonant violinists. I scurried around, battening down possessions, and then rushed to capture an errant bandana just as it flew into the lake. Finally, hunkered down out of the wind behind an enormous boulder, I sat with my bagel, salami, and a scowl, and vowed that when I returned to civilization I would never, ever eat salami again.

It was Labor Day, my teenage daughter's birthday, and I'd had no luck getting cell reception all day. After "dinner," I climbed onto a knoll high above camp and was able to get one measly bar on my phone. If the call worked, I was sure she would be ecstatic to hear my voice! Her wonderful daddy calling, surely the highlight of her birthday. She would have the opportunity to declare her love and gratitude for my making the supreme sacrifice of dragging myself out to the top of this cold, windy rock to call her.

Instead, she sounded distracted—like she was watching TV, eating cake, and wrestling with her sister—while talking to me on the phone. A commercial must have come on because she finally deigned herself to concentrate on the call and say that she was mad that I was camping alone instead of being home celebrating her birthday. Besides, she said, she had seen my backpacking skills and wasn't too sure I was safe by myself (given the events of the last hour, an excellent point). Then when I started to whine—I mean, provide her with details about the challenges of my trip, she said, "Um, Dad, that's great, I gotta go. Bye." Click. Oh sure, go ahead, leave me all alone, go happily about your daily routine, while I am out here living life on the edge, surviving on freaking salami and cheese and my last bagel. Steeling myself for a night of battle against hungry, marauding animals that were trying to fatten up before winter on my leftovers, while the folks on the home front were relaxing, savoring beverages with ice, and enjoying birthday cake. Cold, sweet, carbonated beverages with ice gently clinking against the sides of glasses sounding like birds singing, and tasty morsels of velvety birthday cake melting in their mouth.

Later, inside my tent, I couldn't sleep. The thought of bears finding my food cache was certainly inciting trouble in my brain, as was a sadness that I was here, alone, instead of with my daughter on her birthday. Once I did fall into fitful sleep, I dreamt about laughing squirrels. Those damn laughing squirrels. Don't you just want those poor dogs to catch one for a change? And why does the human whose name I can't remember put up with that nonsense in those *Alvin* movies? I mean, while it's certainly a rarity to own a talking chipmunk, they are still quite obnoxious, and eventually you would think he would figure out it will only end badly. I mean, hasn't he seen the first two movies?

Later, my dreaming moved to playing ultimate Frisbee in a pool, which, when you think about it, has to be pretty challenging, when rain awakened me. Not a drenching "Oh, my God, I need to get up and do something about it" rain. Just a few light drops gently falling onto my face, rousting me from my Frisbee slumber with the thought: "Wait a minute, was that rain?" And another thought: the forecast didn't include rain, so my rain fly was tucked deep into my backpack, which in a fit of animal paranoia I'd hung up high in a tree one hundred yards from my tent. Without a rain fly, that open mesh on the roof of the tent was an enjoyable way to look at stars earlier. Now it was a ready access point for water to hit my face.

A few more lonely drops of wet torture plunked onto my forehead in the pitch-black shortly after five o'clock in the morning. I thought, "Is the rain just getting warmed up and will come down hard soon, or was that the entire rain event and I should just go back to sleep?" Very, very slowly, time passed, until the first hints of gray appeared at the tops of the trees. Every so often, a few more lonely drops would plop into the tent. Each time, I rustled around like a squirrel hiding its nuts, covering up the stuff I really didn't want to get wet. Then the rain would stop, my head would settle back down to the pillow, and I would gaze into the grayness with the sure, gnawing feeling that I am a chump and that I should just do something, but I had no idea what. Finally, I'd had enough. I scrunched and moaned my way out of the tent, dragging cold drops of water from the tent fly all along my back, stumbled in the semidarkness to my backpack, took down my tent, and stuffed all of my crap into my pack. It was time to get the hell out of there.

Then, once the pack was finally synched, I took a deep breath and looked up. A soft, golden glow lit the granite ridgeline. The first rays of sun warmed the smoothed-over ground where my tent used to be, and the cloudless sky was a deep blue. I took another deep breath and caught just a hint of the salty fragrance of wet pine needles and musty rock. Oh, I thought, it's such a delightful morning; I don't have to leave right away. I should relax and make myself a nice breakfast. I hauled all my stuff back out of the bag, set up the stove, and began to boil water for tea and oatmeal. As I waited, a fresh round of clouds swiftly rolled in, and it began to gently rain shortly thereafter. Again.

After several hearty grumbles and "You've got to be kidding me's," I stuffed the pack again and began walking out, which of course made the rain stop and the clouds lift to a gorgeous cerulean sky. The sun was out, but a few drops of rain still fell through the sunshine, miniature rainbows dropping out of the blue. Their mother cloud already flowed on by, set to wet the earth somewhere else. But it was too late to stop again. My mind had already left the wilderness. It was in a restaurant, savoring salty potatoes with fried onions, freshly scrambled eggs, with melted cheese and lovely bits of ham. It was lazily sipping a mocha from a big glass mug, while my butt was comfortably encased in a chair. Over my head, I could see something truly glorious: a roof.

■　■　■

Based on what you've just heard, I'm sure it is hard to believe, but after those first few solo trips I began making plans for a bigger, more challenging solo adventure. Why? It's easy to understand why I would want to get out into the wilderness. I mean, who can resist the allure of waking up to a mountain alive with orange and purple, or watching the day slowly turn to night, while resting on a smooth hunk of granite? I love the purple asters and orange paintbrush fluttering in the wind of a mountain meadow, or floating on my back in an alpine lake watching the clouds slide by soaring, craggy peaks. The wilderness has much to love, and the best way to enjoy it is to spend a few nights following its rhythms and living life on nature's terms. You get so much more out of the experience when you put in the time, instead of just hiking for the day and returning home at night for a shower and turning into a zombie in front of a screen.

But why did I remain so determined to hike solo? Sure, I didn't really have anyone else with whom to hike, I was seeking the peace that only a solo hike could provide, and I was trying to conquer my fears by facing them. But I could also blame it on the time my four older siblings tied me to a tree. When I look back at the incident, what is perhaps most indicative of my future is not that they tied four-year-old me to the tree and then left me there for several hours while they ran off and played, but that I thought it wasn't really that bad to be tied to that tree. It gave me a rare opportunity to enjoy a few hours of peace and quiet.

As the fifth of six kids, I was a teenager when my older sisters were already having kids. My parents were blessed with enough little grandchildren to make Christmas at Tahoe an extremely boisterous affair. I especially remember the year when heavy snow closed the road and kept about twenty of us trapped in my parents' house for three days. Finally, my mom, the grand organizer of all of the family events, and the person for whom the term "Type A" was invented, had had enough. She ran out into the street, screamed, cried, spun around in circles, fainted, then got up, dusted off the snow and came back into the house to again face the onslaught of high-volume, high-pitched voices.

While I can certainly see the appeal of a good meltdown in the middle of the street, from the time I was a little tyke, I preferred solitude as my primary method of escape. In my mind, I was an all-star pitcher, throwing a tennis ball over and over against the stucco retaining wall of our driveway, before I morphed into a Gold Glove shortstop, fielding the grounder and throwing out the fast-moving runner at first base. I believe I threw a few no-hitters against that wall. In the fall, I transformed into a football star, diving across the imaginary goal line time after time and scoring the game-winning touchdown. And of course, there was always the old standby of quietly sneaking into a secluded corner and devouring a book. As a child, my being alone was not something to be sad about; it was accomplishing a challenging goal.

In high school and college, I became more social. I wasn't doing much hiking in those days, unless you count the strenuous walk up the driveway to someone's house for a party. At Chico State in California, my primary form of exercise was riding my bike around campus and playing ultimate Frisbee. The focus was on seeing what happens when you drink copious amounts of alcohol, hanging out with my girlfriend when I had one, or trying to get some girl to go out with me when I didn't, and of course I did some studying (which I actually loved, perhaps because it was something I did quietly by myself).

I was studying to become a city planner, although apparently I was more interested in the studying part than that going to work stuff, so I applied to graduate schools.

Academic standards apparently were lower back then, because somehow I got into grad school at Cornell University in Ithaca, New York. The campus is perched high up on top of the hill overlooking Cayuga Lake and my home in downtown Ithaca. A trail climbed from downtown up a steep gorge to the campus, conquering the hill via a long series of ancient rock steps covered in moss along a roaring stream laced with waterfalls and tumbling cascades. At the end of almost every day, I escaped from Cornell to this enchanting forest tucked in the middle of the city.

After grad school, my first job was for a nonprofit in the Catskill Mountains. I was a single guy in my twenties living in the teensy town of Margaretville, New York. It was the kind of town so sleepy that the newspaper's gossip column was a highlight of the week. My job, however, introduced me to the Catskill 3500 Club. To become a member, you hiked to the top of the thirty-four mountains in the Catskills with summit elevations of more than 3,500 feet. Although I was raised in Tahoe, it was the pursuit of that 3500 Club membership that turned me into a hiker. I was assisted in that effort by a young woman named Linda.

Linda was raised as a member of a large family in a remote part of Upstate New York in a home without TV or radio. Her family hunted deer and raised sheep that they slaughtered themselves. Linda told me that she never tasted beef until she went off to college. While she would always leave me in the dust on the hiking trail, she would inevitably give me a chance to catch up when she stopped to pick up a clump of dried scat on the trail. She would roll it around in her fingers and determine what sort of critter had created it and what it had been eating (and probably how long ago it had eaten). She certainly had no fear of hiking by herself; in fact, she relished it. She knew everything you would need to know to live alone in the Catskill wilderness. When it came to the civilized world, on the other hand, she was certainly out of her realm. I remember this conversation:

ME: "You know, it was a little like that scene from the movie with Humphrey Bogart…"
LINDA: "Who is Humphrey Bogart?"

So she wasn't familiar with American culture. She wasn't much for silly chitter chatter about the non-woods world either. Better that we just shut up and appreciate nature at a fast pace. But she was the first person I had ever met who was totally comfortable being alone in the wilderness for a long period of time, and she made me realize that it was OK to hike by yourself (Linda would later become a New York State wilderness ranger, spending day upon day alone in the wilderness—a job for which she was well suited).

After that, I often solo hiked to check mountains off my 3,500 list. I distinctly remember hiking on my own to the summit of a Catskill peak on a crisp fall day. The forest was a sea of red, yellow, and orange leaves flittering in the soft breeze. The ground was damp, the fallen leaves a musty, muddy reminder that winter was coming. From the summit, I gazed over a vast blanket of color, which looked like crayons melted under wax paper, and realized that I had not seen or heard another person the entire day.

I discovered while hiking in the Catskills that hiking with others is a fun social occasion and an opportunity to learn about and from other people. But the constant chatter changes the hike from intimately connecting with nature to the sensation that you are merely watching a nature video while gabbing away about all things human. The hiking becomes just a pleasant background visual to the conversation. I didn't need to be a hermit and spend twenty years in the Maine woods growing a ZZ Top beard, but in the Catskills I first realized that when you hike alone, you discover much more of what nature had to give and are given the opportunity to truly absorb those gifts.

After I finished hiking the thirty-four Catskill peaks and became member No. 512 of the Catskill 3500 Club, my boss said that if I only had as much devotion to my job as I did to hiking every weekend, he wouldn't have had to let me go. The good news is the loss of my job meant it was time to move back home to Tahoe, and as soon as I made it home I found I had a new appreciation for the place where I had been raised. It was now a place to hike, and I was ready to hike. After some slightly frumpy years in college, I was in pretty good hiking shape. Sure, still short and nearly blind without my glasses, but strong enough to take on some lengthy jaunts.

I trekked to the top of Mount Tallac, where in one direction nearly all the vast deep blue of Lake Tahoe unfolds below and a quick spin reveals the sparkling shimmer of Gilmore Lake, Susie Lake, and a sliver of Lake Aloha, dwarfed by the unbroken mass of granite that is the Crystal Range. On another day, I topped a giant boulder on the Rubicon Trail, where I watched ospreys screech and bump up against bald eagles, fighting for territory above the emerald green and intensely blue waters of Lake Tahoe.

       ■ ■ ■

Hiking solo not only helped me to focus on what I saw in nature, but it also gave my brain a chance to push the reset button before the jumble of civilization had a chance to drive me batty. When I became a writer, I quickly discovered that if I wanted to get a new idea or work through a writing challenge, I needed to head out the door, preferably for the whole day, to let my mind pop out the answers. Most often the answers would come, or a new and interesting idea that needed to be written would burst into my consciousness. It was all about giving my brain a chance to wander without being tied down to one thought. And if I hiked all day and had nothing insightful to show for it, who cares? A day of hiking is still the best therapy.

3

Six Days on the John Muir Trail

How truly glorious the landscape circled around this
noble summit!—Giant mountains, valleys innumerable,
glaciers and meadows, rivers and lakes, with
the wide blue sky bent tenderly over them all.

—John Muir

WITH A NEWFOUND, and perhaps ill-founded, devotion to the power of solo backpacking to soothe my soul, I planned a six-day trip that included a portion of the John Muir Trail (JMT). I was seeking a direct connection with nature that I only find when I hike in silence. Sure, when I'm alone in the wilderness, lots of sounds surround me: the cornflake crunch as my feet touch the ground, the intricate symphony of the birds whistling in the aspen trees, the gentle roar of a creek filled with melting snow, or the rush of wind moving through pine needles. But these are the sounds of nature, which magically bring me to a place where the inner and outer sounds of civilization disappear. Not the clamor of cars roaring by my house, or the guttural midnight howl of that loud neighbor who has had just a few dozen too many. More importantly, the pesky sounds inside my noggin drift away as my crunching feet saunter down the trail. Given enough alone time in nature, I no longer try to remember if I paid that insurance bill, if the house needs a coat of paint, or whether that guy up the street will ever stop yelling.

When hiking with others, I feel as if I'm cruising over the scene in a drone, capturing live coverage of the event for the TV Tim channel inside my head. When alone in the wilderness, however, I become an actual character in the show, as much a part of the scene as the ant crawling up my leg and the pine needles fluttering in the breeze.

■ ■ ■

The 211-mile-long John Muir Trail was the brainchild of Theodore Solomons, obviously a total slacker, who in 1884 at the ripe old age of fourteen began advocating for a hiking trail between Yosemite Valley and Mount Whitney in the Sierra Nevada. Solomons was the fifth of seven children, and his great-grandfather was the first native-born rabbi in the United States. When the Sierra Club was formed in 1892, with John Muir as its first president, Solomons joined the new organization and set off to explore much of the largely unexplored High Sierra in hopes of developing the route for a trail. Solomons met Muir several times, saying, "Muir was exceedingly generous in his encouragement of us younger mountaineers, he gave us much time, and was patient with our fool questions."

In what is now the Evolution Valley area, Solomons discovered and named six peaks after famous evolutionists, including Mount Darwin after Charles Darwin, who had died only ten years earlier. Apparently, Solomons was quite smitten with Darwin's scientific theories. By 1896, he had completed an accurate map of the Sierra, which along with a great deal of exploration by Joseph Le Conte, led to the alignment of the trail.

■ ■ ■

Originally to be called the High Sierra Trail, the trail later became a memorial to John Muir, who died in 1914. Construction began in 1915, and it wasn't completed until 1938. The builders, primarily crews hired by the United States Forest Service and National Park Service, had a lot to overcome, including steep, high-altitude terrain that was prone to avalanche. Accessing the trail route for resupplies was a long and challenging journey, and construction season only ran from when the snow finally melted in July to when it started snowing again, often as early as September. The last two sections to be built were the most difficult: Forester Pass, which was conquered in 1932, and Palisade Creek, near Mather Pass, finished in 1938. The JMT crosses through three national parks, and a hiker who completes the whole trail will face more than 47,000 feet of elevation gain.

DAY ONE

It was a Dusy.

For twenty minutes I'd been standing, shuffling my feet atop the dry roadside at the edge of the trailhead parking lot. I was ready to stick my thumb out, but not a single car had passed. One of those crooked light bulbs was slowly starting to illuminate in my brain that there might be a kink in what I thought was a stunningly brilliant shuttle plan. I'd been hoping for a ride from the North Lake Trailhead to South Lake Trailhead. I had picked these trailheads, on the east side of the Sierra Nevada near Bishop, California, because even though they were only about ten miles apart, they allowed for a breathtaking, nearly sixty-mile loop through the heart of the High Sierra wilderness, including a particularly attractive portion of the JMT.

Now I was slowly remembering an important rule of trailhead usage: people rarely exit a remote hiking trailhead at eight o'clock in the morning, since to get to said trailhead by that time they would have to wake up at ungodly a.m., when it is freaking cold, pack up their camp, and hike out miles of difficult trail to get to the trailhead by eight. What is the hurry? Instead, while I stood there waiting, most hikers were happily snoring away or waiting for it to get warmer before they'd be willing to dip a toe out of their tent. Even the early birds would be quietly contemplating the view of the mountains while nursing a cup of cocoa.

While it's OK to depend upon the kindness of strangers, for the concept to work, you have to actually create the opportunity to encounter a kind stranger. My hopes of getting over the substantial climb to Bishop Pass and then down into the lower and safer elevations before the threatening afternoon thunderstorms were beginning to look at this point like a mere dream.

This trip, if it would ever get started, was just my second lengthy foray into the High Sierra, the area between Yosemite and Mount Whitney, where all of the Sierra's 14,000-foot peaks are. My first hike was several years earlier, also on the JMT, a five-day trip with my friend Karen starting at Cottonwood Pass south of Mount Whitney. She was hiking the entire JMT and had arranged to have a number of different folks hike sections with her. On my last day, while I headed out over Kearsage Pass carrying her trash, her husband was heading in to meet her with a fresh supply of food.

On that trip, I first discovered the vastness of the Southern Sierra wilderness and the amazing feat it was to create this trail in such foreboding terrain of sharp, high peaks and steep canyons. We spent every night above 10,000 feet, surrounded by mountains reaching several thousand feet higher. The sheer scale of the mountains and valleys both stunned and intimidated me. My heart frequently skipped beats partly because of the dizzying immenseness of it, but also because of my fear of heights. Sure, the actual walking along cliff edges made my head spin, stomach flutter, and mind angry at myself for letting the fear of heights get to me, but these intervals of terror were fairly short. Most frustrating was that I let my fear of future scary sections take away from what should have been my focus now: the natural splendor in front of my face.

The third night we camped in a treeless high plain beside a glacial tarn. Surrounded by lush, short grasses, the tarn set like a well-manicured water feature on the world's highest golf course. After several hours frolicking in its relatively warm waters, we relaxed on the grass and contemplated our incredible luck at being there. The high ridgeline to the east was just transitioning to evening pink. It was topped by Mount Whitney, the Lower 48s' highest peak, which appeared as just another rocky blip along the immense ridge.

On the fourth day, Karen and I crossed over Forester Pass, at 13,153 feet, the highest pass on the JMT north of Mount Whitney and the highest elevation on the 2,600-mile-long Pacific Crest Trail (PCT). I'd made the mistake of reading the guidebook trail description several days before approaching the pass, which to me read like a horror novel. It recounted in detail that the trail was dynamited out of the sheer rock face, creating a narrow, cliff-edgy ascent to the pass. Near the top, I trudged along the precipice tentatively, head and stomach spinning, feet sweating, eyes firmly focused on the ground in front of my feet, hoping that the next step would not send me flying off the trail and into the ether. Meanwhile, Karen kept blabbing and pointing, "Wow, look at that over there!"

Look up? Are you fucking kidding me? Eventually, I reached the cold pass, drenched in the sweat of fear. Standing at the top were a father and his smiling eight-year-old son, who thought hiking up this pass was really fun.

■ ■ ■

When I was back on the lonely road next to the North Lake trailhead, a rusty pickup truck rolled to a stop in front of me. A middle-aged cowboy leaned out the window and told me to hop in. He owned the local pack stables, and his horses had been hauling hundreds of pounds of supplies to campers in the heart of this wilderness for more than thirty years. I wondered how many of the luscious, quiet hours that I was seeking he had enjoyed over all those years? Horse packing is somewhat of an endangered occupation in the High Sierra, since every season might bring another new crop of government restrictions, making it harder for packing operations to stay in business. Eventually, horses will probably be gone from the wilderness except for trail maintenance. Unfortunately, this will eliminate the opportunity for folks who can't carry a heavy pack to get into the remote wilderness. It will also make more rare the sight of a cowboy or cowgirl riding into the sunset—an important part of the history and allure of the western wilderness.

My second ride, which brought me to the trailhead, came from two younger guys who were heading out to chew up a lot of miles on a four-day hike. Trying not to delay them, I struggled to quickly wrench my always-too-heavy pack into the only remaining space in their packed-to-the-gills truck bed when a sharp pain shot up my back. For the rest of the day, the spasm was like a toddler who can't stop asking questions: no matter how hard you try, there is no way you are going to be able to forget that she is there.

As I struggled to reacquaint myself with the pain of hiking up a Southern Sierra pass, I was also growing to understand why Muir spent so much time exploring the high peaks of the Sierra. The air is refreshingly clean, with a translucent light that leads to an impossibly blue sky. Below, immense, craggy peaks rise to well above the tree line, with sheer, snowcapped summits. Equally enticing are the spaces in between all that rock—narrow canyons with waves of conifers shoving against sparkling green meadows dotted with purple lupine and orange paintbrush. Then there are the shimmering lakes, tiny gems with crystal-clear water, enticing tired hikers in for a swim, then quickly reminding those hikers that these lakes are laden with recently melted snow and are thus tremendously cold.

■　■　■

"Yeah, but Johnny boy…. Muir dude. Yo. How come we don't hear tales of how your back or hips hurt while you were hiking in the middle of nowhere and sleeping on the ground, or how you forgot to bring your biscuits and nearly starved to death, or how the water you drank out of that creek had some nasty critters in it that left you paying the price for the next two weeks with quick trips for relief behind the bushes? Eh? Or maybe, just maybe, even though you loved being out there alone, that sometimes you got lonely? Cuz, Mr. Muir, I was definitely paying a price for all that beauty."

On the first day, the fare was a grueling 2,100-foot climb to the top of rocky 11,972-foot Bishop Pass. Every time I looked the wrong way, the spasms jumped up and said, "Howdy doody." The hips and shoulders and feet shouted, "What the hell? Why are we doing this again?" Then I crossed over the pass into Kings Canyon National Park, the promised land, the grand entrance into the vast expanse of wilderness of the Southern Sierra that would be my home for a few days, and all was somewhat forgiven. From the top, I skipped along a gentle 1,200-foot descent over sandy, decomposed granite past gnarly whitebark pines and smooth boulders to a large shallow lake in the desolate Dusy Basin.

Thanks to early explorers' great deal of forethought and romance, the lake next to where I camped was given the majestic name: 10,742. When I realize how many delightful lakes and peaks in the Sierra still have names like 10,742 (the lake's elevation), it heartens me that perhaps there are still unexplored, or at least lightly explored, places out there. Our lives are short and there is so much to see, and we spend way too much time staring at screens. All we can do is keep moving forward, trying new things, and keep heading back into paradise as often as possible.

Later, I rest in my tent, listening to the pattering of rain and loud crackles of thunder, while counting the seconds between the shafts of blinding light and the boom of the strike. Wait, was it one second equals a mile or a quarter mile? And how many Mississippis equal a second? In between counting, I thought about food, and how it would be nice to have time before dark to escape the tent and fix dinner. It's quite amazing that I love backpacking, since one of life's great pleasures is food. While one of my primary objectives is making sure I am able to stuff copious quantities of food into my mouth on a regular basis, I also enjoy the tasty stuff. There is absolutely no tasty stuff on a backpacking trip. Well, to be honest, there could be tasty stuff if you wanted to take the time and energy to cook, stir, simmer, add things, follow recipes, and all that, and then later clean up the awful mess at a campsite. Eww. No thanks. For me, the extent of my cooking on a backpack trip will always be to boil water, pour it into a foil pouch, and then wait for the often-bland food to become edible.

While I will admit that eating one of those dehydrated chili mac and cheese specials tastes considerably better on the edge of a lake while you watch the sun slowly dip behind a mountain peak than it would at the dining room table, it will still never be gourmet. And no matter how exotic your wilderness locale, dehydrated ice cream will never be ice cream. It's Styrofoam with a hint of chocolate.

■ ■ ■

After the afternoon thunderstorms blew away, I tried to relax my back spasms by lying on a smooth patch of granite next to the shore and watched the 13,000-foot peaks that surround Dusy Basin first turn orange, then transition to bright red. I heard the distant rumble of falling rocks, slowly adding to the immense talus fields at the base of the sheer pinnacles of granite.

The wispy sound of waterfalls carried to me on the cool night wind. I heard the soft plop of fish jumping and tent flaps gently rustling. Chickadees chirped from branch to branch, while frogs started croaking evening greetings. OK, stop…hope you enjoyed that idyllic evening interlude as much as I did, because soon the wind roared up the canyon, violently rattling the formerly docile tent flaps, and dark clouds flowed over The Lake Known As 10,742. I scampered into the tent and frantically zipped up the rain fly as the first drops pattered the roof. A bright flash of light, a brief lull, then a thunderous boom, another pregnant pause, and the final release of rain—all of it, a deluge. And me, inside, hunkered down, trying to become invisible to the lightning gods as rivulets of rushing water flowed around and under the tent. I finger-poked the tent bottom, and it rippled back like my old college waterbed. It was then I remembered that I needed to take a leak.

Sure, I could wait, but it dawned on me that if a flash of lightning got too close it might scare the piss out of me. So I doffed my clothes (why get them wet too?), and dashed outside. Instantly I was soaking wet, freezing cold, and feeling like I was in every movie where someone was desperately searching for their lost love in the rain. And now, like a biathlete getting his heart rate down from all that cross-country skiing to be able to shoot the target, I attempted to relax so the plumbing would work and I could create my own mini rainstorm. When it finally happened, it did feel pretty good. I might have yeehawed.

DAY TWO ▪ Down, down, down…up, up, up.
Camp at Lake 10,800 feet

When the sun rose, I peeked outside my tent: steam rising from little puddles, tent dripping and splattered with mud. Inside: sleeping bag a warm, dry cocoon. It would take some gumption to get out of that comfy bag and face the mess outside. While I did not have the ambition to conquer Everest, I did want to succeed, whatever that is. And I did have an anxious curiosity to see what natural delight awaits me on the next mile.

So I raised myself out of the warmth and into the wet, and began the after-a-deluge drying-out process. This procedure, with which every backpacker who ever camps in the rain quickly becomes familiar, involves placing every wet thing on smooth rocks, watching anxiously, and desperately hoping that the sun and breeze will dry them. Fortunately for Sierra hikers, the mountain air is as dry as a crinkly mule's ear flower in October and things do dry, though never fast enough.

Day Two's hiking began with a seemingly unending series of switchbacks descending the steep slope into Le Conte Canyon (yes, the same Le Conte who planned the route for this trail, and who also has a lake named after him in Desolation Wilderness near the Tahoe Rim Trail). Passing great boulders that seemed to have been tossed haphazardly across the trail by a giant, I gingerly worked down the slant, serenaded by the gentle rustle of a thin cascade bustling its way down the smooth granite wall all the way to the distant bottom of the canyon.

I stopped for a break and looked across the deep divide at the utterly imposing rock massive on the other side and wondered: how could it be possible that my next major challenge, Muir Pass, is in the middle of that huge conglomeration of rock? When you have spent most of your hiking days in the rounded, user-friendly, never-more-than-10,000-foot-high mountains around Lake Tahoe, the sheer immenseness of the rocky peaks in the Southern Sierra are daunting. It just does not seem possible that a trail could be built through that seemingly impenetrable wall of stone in front of you, but somehow the trail snakes its way around this mountain, then slowly wiggles its way around that steep cliff, to reach the pass. One fortunate rule of thumb for hiking on popular trails in the high mountains is that the trail on which you are about to embark is probably not as difficult or as steep as it looks from a distance. Which is a good thing, because some of them look more difficult than getting Congress to cut spending.

I set up camp next to a sheet of deep-blue water surrounded by high rocky crags. The wind was chilly and the lake placidly stark with just a few weather-beaten whitebark pines hanging onto their last refuge just below the tree line. Across the valley was the Black Divide, several of the few remaining High Sierra glaciers clinging to its north-facing cliff. Looking at glaciers in the Sierra is like stepping back in time, the remnant of the most recent ice age, hanging on precariously over thousands of years. There is a certain timelessness to the ice, a depth and a translucent color that sets it apart from the ordinary snowfields surrounding it. While they appear timeless, the glaciers are also a reminder of the ever-changing character of the earth's landscape. Thousands of years ago, most of these mountains were buried underneath dense glaciers, and at some point in the future, the cycle will most likely renew and the glaciers will return again with the next ice age. Millions of years ago, where we walk today was under a great ocean and eventually will be under the ocean again. While we use the term "rock solid" to describe the unchanging character of land, in the long term what we see as the landscape is very transient. It's like a movie—the kind they used to make with actual film—and the entire history of human civilization is depicted in just one frame.

* * *

My tent sat smack in the middle of what appeared to be a Southern Sierra Chamber of Commerce brochure; just looking at it, you couldn't help but gasp "Gollliee!" and "Will you look at that!" It sounded good too, with the relaxing babble of the creek draining the lake just down the slope from my tent. After I settled in, a group of campers arrived and plunked down an "insta home" just a stone's throw away. I was undecided whether I felt relief that humans were there in case of an emergency or bummed that once again my quiet connection to the mountains was temporarily severed. In reality, though, after spending the day dropping almost 3,000 feet, only to climb right back up to the same elevation at which I had started, I was too pooped to sincerely analyze my philosophy of hiking alone.

Instead, I realized that I saw more waterfalls and water cascading down steep slopes that day than I had in my entire life. Each watercourse put forth its best effort to be the most spectacular.

■ ■ ■

The best times in the backcountry are the early morning and early evening, when the lighting is at its most captivating. A certain calming quiet of such special light relaxes and connects me to the natural world. At dawn, I watch the golden sun slowly march across the rock, happily anticipating the moment it reaches my campsite, warming the air and my heart. At the end of the day, the light slowly dies, imparting a delicate, surreal appeal to the landscape that feels like a relaxing Savasana, bringing me gently into the night. On my second night, after the sun had departed from my lake, an orange glow rimmed the knife edge of the nearby mountain. It was as if someone had taken a crayon and drawn a bright-orange border along the edge of the ridgeline. A mountain halo, smudged up tight against the rock, reminded me of the spiritual power of being in this place where nature is in control.

DAY THREE ▪ Finding Paradise through Evolution.
Campsite, Evolution Lake

This may be the most spectacular and varied lake along the route. It's dotted with miniature rock islands, most sporting a few whitebark pines, with huge rock precipices and even loftier peaks reaching higher still, as a backdrop. Near my campsite, a waterfall plunged down the steep embankment toward the green meadows of Evolution Valley far below. My tent sat in a large, flat area at the end of a peninsula that juts into the lake. I scrubbed clothes in my bear canister, and they dried on the warm granite in the midday sun while I swam in the warmest lake yet this trip (but still icy cold). Even though the pit of loneliness and nagging sore muscles were companions, the glory of the day's journey washed away despair and replaced it with a joyful heart full of wonder and gratitude. While I can't match Muir's seemingly boundless optimism in the wilderness, I wholly identify with his appreciation for the power of nature to soothe our souls and to remind us how lucky we are to be alive, and in this place.

While strolling past the series of lakes sitting in the open, rocky basin below Muir Pass, a fellow hiker seeking food approached me. Since I'd begun to realize I had too much food and he had too little, we had the makings of a win-win situation. He received the sustenance that he obviously needed, and I was rewarded with something even more valuable: less weight. Should I feel satisfied that I did a good deed in helping a hungry stranger, or guilty because I chose to pass on the heaviest food item in my pack? As I walked away, though, I became curious. Was he just a bit short of food, or did he head off into the woods with the plan to live totally off the kindness of strangers? If it was the latter, I am not sure if I am impressed with the size of his gonads or startled by his stupidity.

Later in the day, two lone hikers reached the lake and we gathered for a visit (people hiking alone tend to alternate between being outgoing and being reclusive). They ended up camping with me on my peninsula (I was the first one there, so for that night it was *my* peninsula), and we spent the evening telling each other our stories. After a few days alone, talking to people beats talking to yourself, although there are situations in which talking to yourself is preferred. A principle I was reminded of the following day.

Raj was doing the entire John Muir Trail and had about eight days left. Julie was hiking the same loop I was, but in the opposite direction. So while Julie and I regaled each other with what we each would experience on the trail over the next three days, Raj informed us that his preferred method of protecting his food from bears was to bring it into his tent with him. While Sierra black bears are wary of humans, they also suffer from a severe obsession with food and would have no trouble taking it away from him and, perhaps, purely by accident, a portion of his tent and an arm or two as well. Most alarming for me was the thought that once said bear discovered that tents are just grocery bags, he might think the next tent, say mine, for example, might also contain lots of tasty tidbits. The thought came to me that comes to all of us at least several times a day when we are watching the behavior of other humans: "What in the hell is he thinking?"

What seems especially interesting about this trail is everyone's willingness, even eagerness, to stop and chat, or camp next to each other, or give away food (take some of my food, please). A real spirit of togetherness seems to increase the farther you are from the trailhead. It's as if you know that you may need these people. Or perhaps it is better than that. When life is simple and you are not directly tied into the cord of constant communication, you enjoy meeting and talking with people you don't know and having real conversations.

Long-distance hikers who have escaped the need to stop every ten minutes and text, "I'm here now…where are you?" can more easily relate to other human beings face to face. And of course if they still have difficulty learning how to talk to other humans, the lack of cell reception in the wilderness helps them.

I've also noticed that the smaller the group, the more chatty people are. If you pass ten people walking together on the trail, you will get just a perfunctory hello. They have brought their companionship with them and don't need to seek it from you. The lone hiker, however, is more ready to find conversation and companionship from other solo hikers.

DAY FOUR ▪ Escaping Evolution

Lunch in Evolution Valley

After leaving Evolution Lake, I dropped to a glorious set of bright-green meadows that make up Evolution Valley, progressing slowly toward Goddard Canyon. After the grueling climbs of the past three days, spending a few hours walking easily through a sparkling wave of green was a relief. On a sandbar in Evolution Meadow, the lowest of the three meadows, I had a quiet lunch on the edge of the gently flowing river.

OK, to be honest, I was not just sitting on that sandbar because I thought it would make a nice place to dine. I was hiding behind my backpack, trying to stay perfectly still so I wouldn't attract attention, looking away from the trail to avoid eye contact with a particular hiker who I was afraid would be coming by soon.

It had begun an hour earlier. I strolled by a fellow who was standing just a few feet off the side of the trail cowering in the trees. I gave him a fleeting hello, and he stepped right behind me onto the trail. He began blabbering a nonstop litany of complaints and nonsensical utterances for the next twenty minutes as he walked so closely behind me that if I stopped he would have run into me. I believe I may have gotten in one "Hummm" and a "Really?" but mainly I was just being treated to the extended playlist on Radio Station Whacko. Eventually, he stopped to talk to someone else hiking in the opposite direction, and I saw my opportunity for escape. I stepped on the gas and walked swiftly away down the trail. I briefly felt guilty, though I'm not sure whether I felt guilty for abandoning him or the poor guy who was stuck talking to him, but thought it was better than running into the woods screaming and throwing my arms up in the air. You know, becoming him or my poor mom surrounded by all those grandkids at Christmastime. Perhaps this is just nature's way of reminding me that being alone really does have its benefits—you only have the crazy person in your head to worry about. Those cozy, familiar thought patterns with which you hopefully have developed a means of coping.

■ ■ ■

After lunch, I tentatively stepped back onto the trail, looked in both directions, then snuck out of Evolution Valley, stopping frequently to double-check that I was alone and that pesky guy wasn't lurking in the trees. It's a good thing no one was watching, because my frequent stops to look about anxiously in all directions might have made me look suspicious. After just a few days on the JMT, it certainly seemed plausible that there would be more than one guy like him on this trail.

By late afternoon, it was blazing hot when I reached the junction of the John Muir and Piute Pass Trails, my planned campsite for the evening. I found soft ground covered in a blanket of pine needles along a swiftly moving creek. A pleasant setting, but after the windswept whitebark pines and rock slabs butting against azure lakeshores of the campsites above 10,000 feet, it was a letdown to have dropped down to 8,000 feet, a land of pine duff, dusty trails, and bears.

Noticing numerous broken ropes twisting in the wind above my tent made me ponder the bears. The logical conclusion to seeing the series of ripped cords hanging from trees: hikers incorrectly hung their food just before dark, couldn't figure out how to get the rope down in the morning, and then ferociously hacked at the rope with their puny backpacking knifes. But the emotional/fearful part of my personality is drawn to a more suspenseful explanation: a marauding bear tromped into camp, and as the children screamed and parents stood dumbfounded with deer-in-the-headlights looks, the bear reached up with its enormous claws, ripped down the food bags, and then devoured everything inside. Next it wandered around the camp to see what other food might be found. It's always a good idea to try to come up with something pleasant to think about just before dipping into my tent.

As is often the case when I'm tired and hungry, which I always am when backpacking, I put those fears to rest, settled down to watch the sunset, and hummed the famous tune from *Jeopardy!* for fifteen minutes while waiting patiently for my meal to cook in its pouch. When the magic moment finally arrived, I salivated with anticipation of that first savory spoonful. I took a big bite and instantly my mouth exploded with a firecracker of painful, spicy heat. I desperately dove for the water bottle and quickly slurped down several gulps... nope, that didn't work. Still scorching. Then, failing to remember that the definition of insanity is doing the same thing over and over again and expecting a different result, I took another bite. Nope, still freaking hot.

What do I do with this stuff? I started accosting passing hikers who were unlucky enough to be walking by with an offer of a free meal. It's hard to understand why they wouldn't jump at the opportunity to receive a partially eaten firecracker of a meal offered by a man who smelled like he'd been hiking for two weeks and had flames coming out of his mouth. They looked at me, raised their eyebrows in alarm, then walked swiftly away, turning around for a quick glance to make sure I wasn't following, then sped up again. Perhaps they thought I was another unstable guy on the trail, like the one that attempted to talk their ears off earlier in the day in Evolution Valley. Fortunately, I did discover that acting loony led any potential fellow campers to skedaddle on down the trail in search of a saner place to camp.

After failing to pass my spicy problem off to someone else, I climbed up the side of the mountain and stuffed the globby remains in a deep hole. This burying food ritual was beginning to get old. The only salient part of the experience is that I had hoped a chipmunk would discover the cache, chow down heartily, and then spin around in circles with his mouth aflame like me. Would he then swear off human food for the duration? If so, perhaps I should be carrying a jar of Tabasco with me on camping trips to keep the little bastards at bay.

DAY FIVE ▪ A Long One
Oops, Humphreys just went right on by.

Despite my fears, the evening transpired bearless. The next day would end up being the most strenuous day of the trip, with a 3,400-foot climb to the top of Piute Pass. With four days under my belt, much of it spent extensively daydreaming about eating hamburgers and drinking milkshakes, I was able to occasionally reach a state of walking meditation. Backpacking makes me crave meat and chocolate. Not sure if the craving for meat comes from burning all those calories or if it is caused by the frustrating tease of only getting three corn-kernel-sized bits of chicken in my freeze-dried backpack dinner. When it comes to the chocolate milkshake, that craving is more straight-forward: "Hi, my name is Tim…and I'm a chocoholic."

The plan for Day Five was to hike into Humphreys Basin and find my dream campsite next to a creek. Exhausted and slightly delirious, I stumbled into the basin at four in the afternoon, finding a lunar landscape of granite boulders haphazardly tossed around a stark, almost treeless valley. With a bitter wind roaring across the open plain, I stopped behind a beaten-down bush, put on another layer, took another look at the barren landscape, and trudged right through the basin without stopping to camp.

I'm not exactly sure why Humphreys didn't hit my joy button; it sure looks "purdy" in the pictures. Perhaps I'd been hiking so long I'd reached the "there is no way to stop this train" mode. What guys do stereotypically when they are supposed to ask for directions or find a place to stop for dinner. I kept ascending, kept slowly plod-ding, all the way to the top of the almost 11,500-foot-high Piute Pass. From there, I descended to Piute Lake, which sat in an open, rocky flat with high stark peaks rising immediately from its southern shore. I set up camp near a few krummholz whitebark pines that held tight to the ground, hiding from the ferocious storms regularly roaring down from the pass.

Staring at the lake, facing a biting wind that would freeze the balls off the devil, I decided that of course I had to get in. It was a lake. I'd been hiking for five days. It is what needed to be done. Swim-ming, however, would not be the appropriate term. I plunged in with gasps and squeaks, quickly dunked my head while hyperventilating, thrashed my arms around a few times in an attempt to start breath-ing again, and rushed out as fast as bare feet on slippery, sharp rocks would allow. As I lay shivering on cold stone, I thought that perhaps a person of more intelligence might have stayed out of the water. I'd heard of people getting hypothermia from accidentally falling into freezing water, but I'd never heard of people getting hypothermia after jumping into freezing water on purpose. Apparently, the idiots who have done such a thing either died before they had to tell their story, or just lied to the emergency personnel to avoid the embarrassment.

With numb, trembling fingers, I rushed to boil water to create some warmth. I neglected to open up the third leg of the stove, however, and discovered a basic principle of physics: when you open up only two of the three legs of a three-legged stove, water falls over. To make matters worse, before placing the water on the two-legged stove, I had put the spice powder and olive oil for my couscous feast in the pot. When it splatted to the ground, it made a wonderful-smelling sandy mess and put the kibosh on my plans for a couscous meal. What time did that hamburger place in Bishop close, and would it be worth walking out in the dark? Am I capable of actually preparing a dinner? It was then that I realized that while raw vegans may try to make you believe they do it because of their health or ethical considerations, I'm thinking they are just people who couldn't figure out how to operate cooking devices.

Fortunately, tucked in the deepest dredges of the bear canister, was an emergency packet of ramen noodles, which was a good thing, since the raw vegan lifestyle has never appealed to me. If you pick your time and place correctly, a twenty-cent ramen dinner can be a glorious feast. I wolfed it down, then dove into my sleeping bag in a valiant effort to stop the shivering. One does not fully appreciate the pure joy of a down sleeping bag until its primary purpose is as refuge from the bitter cold. Comfortably ensconced in my bag, I found it still early enough in the evening to jot down some summary reflections on my trip:

> I have seen some incredible sights, while learning a lot about myself, but I'm now ready to hightail it out of here and get home. Backpacking is really hard on the back, the hips, the shoulders, and the legs. It is hard to sleep on the ground in the cold, thinking about bears, and it can be lonely. On the other hand, you go to places that you would never see otherwise. Sensationally gorgeous places that will take your breath away, where the only sounds you hear are the wind, water, birds, marmots, and squirrels. You really do get the opportunity to escape from reality and meditate on your existence. Actually, one might argue that you escape to reality—and escape from our artificial world. The world of civilization may be where we spend the most time, but the natural world is who we really are deep in our souls. You will never feel more alive than when you are on a long-distance backpack trip, even though at the end of each day you may feel like you are ready to die.

DAY SIX

The last day

I woke up early to a dark sky, impending rain, and a sense that I'd experienced this before as I confronted questions I'd asked myself at Middle Velma Lake, when those first drops of rain plopped into my tent the year before. Will it rain? Should I get up and put on the rain fly? So hey, why didn't I put on the fly last night before I went to bed instead of having to do it in the dark once the rain had started to fall and it's bone-chilling cold out there? Because I had finally found warmth, and it would have taken a bear to drag me out of my sleeping bag cocoon of comfort. It's like at home, when you are in bed, just turned out the light, laid your head on the pillow, shut your eyes, and then...Wait! "Did I lock the door? Did I turn off the stove?" You really, really do not want to give up the warmth, and you know that 99 percent of the time you did lock it up or turn it off. Now take that scenario and understand that the temperature outside your bed was twenty degrees.

Once it was light enough to see, I rolled out of the tent and skittered around, putting away my camp, stopping every few minutes to rub my frosty hands together. The sky was not as ominous as it appeared with the first gray of morning, but the temperature was certainly brisk enough to get my butt in gear. I hiked out quickly, like a horse on its way back to the barn. The bright-orange Piute Crags were aglow in the morning sun. I passed shiny white aspen groves, leaves quaking in the breeze, and a brisk stream bustling through a deep-green forest. But I didn't really appreciate any of that—I was hell-bent for home. When I began my day at 11,000 feet, the temperature was in the low twenties. When I reached Bishop at 4,000 feet in Owens Valley, it was close to noon, and baking in the mid-eighties. Even though I had spent days dreaming of burgers, the draw of home was even more powerful, and perhaps my stench was equally compelling, so I headed north for home.

■   ■   ■

Life was good. My Subie was rolling down the empty highway through the open sage of the Eastern Sierra toward a warm shower and a soft bed. Home: a place where you can touch a handle and water comes out, where you can sit down, relax, take a dump, and not have to then cover it up with a shovel.

I had a full tank of gas, a bottle of ice-cold orange juice, and Led Zeppelin was rockin' about "lonely, lonely, lonely times" on my CD player. All was well until…five miles north of Bishop: that sinking, helpless feeling that life was about to suck, and the air was about to disappear from my Zeppelin. A flat tire. As I stood caramelizing on the blazing asphalt and trying to conjure air into the flattened piece of rubber, I was finding it hard to fathom that a few hours earlier I was freezing my ass off next to a mountain lake. I was once again reminded that life is just like backpacking. It's a mixture of joy and pain…sometimes within just a few minutes of each other.

Later, as I was rolling into a Bishop tire store in a AAA tow truck, I told myself that of course the reason I got a flat tire was that the dream of a burger, fries, and a shake cannot be denied. So, to prevent an additional catastrophe, I went to Bill's BBQ and loaded up on the essential ingredients that would allow me to continue my journey home. With a full belly, I headed north again. All I needed to rescue my day was a nice patch of water to jump into, something to take a bit of an edge off the sour reek emanating from my body and hopefully rejuvenate my flat-tired brain. I was aware that Bishop is right on the edge of the desert and that most of the sparkling snowmelt that comes down from the mountains was now sitting in swimming pools and washing cars in Los Angeles, but I had hope that I would find an oasis.

Then, there it was. Just a few miles north of Bishop, out of the corner of my eye, I caught a large informational sign. It touted a county park with a series of those symbols for all of the wonderful things available for recent mountain refugees to use. The only sign I really paid attention to was the universally recognized and glorious depiction of what looks like a one-armed swimmer pulling through the water. The swimmer's face was not visible, but he or she was obviously smiling and enjoying a nice, long dip in an awesomely clean and cool body of water. I drove into this oasis of green in the brown of Owens Valley and thought I had arrived at my Shangri-la. There were moist, impeccably manicured lawns and a large, inviting pond with tall, scattered palm trees along the shoreline. Not that the observation would have stopped me, but later I realized that no one else was swimming in the pond and there were swim-at-your-risk signs. A bathroom and changing room stood right next to the pond, so it had to be OK.

I donned a suit and waved happily at the large family who were enjoying a picnic at a table. I tiptoed a few steps onto a little sandbar, the refreshingly cool water rinsing the pain from my toes. "Ah, this is more like it," I thought with a big grin. Then I took the next step, from yellow sand into dark-brown dirt. Immediately, I was two-feet deep into a thick quicksand of muddy goop. As I struggled to escape, I only dug myself deeper into the sticky brown ooze, now reaching up to my hips. Amid the sounds of my splashing and flailing, I could hear the faint sound of laughter from the picnicking family. They probably couldn't believe someone was stupid enough to try to swim in this mudhole. I'm sure they were shaking their heads and quietly saying, "tourons!"

I struggled for a few more minutes, frantically trying to extricate myself from the slop, then took a deep breath and decided I might as well relax and enjoy the comforting feeling of being incased in wet mud. People pay good money for mud baths in Napa Valley, and I'm getting one for free. Then I started to laugh. There is no way around it. Stuff was just going to happen to me. I looked at the still-laughing family on the shoreline and felt proud. At least I had made their day.

Why we backpack...to be here after the sun goes down.

Sauntering down the not-scary side of Forester Pass.

Relief after having just conquered the scary side of Forester Pass.

A spectacular tarn along the John Muir Trail.

Idyllic Evolution Valley, but watch out for strange people.

At Muir Pass, about to descend into Evolution Basin and Evolution Lake and the middle of nowhere.

Lonely paradise at Le Conte Canyon on the John Muir Trail.

Dusy Basin—and the rain begins to come down...

Tahoe Rim Trail—seeing where you have been and how many miles you still have to go.

Star Lake—first lake on the trail, hallelujah.

Showers Lake—another beautiful lake, if only I'd stayed there.

Lake Aloha—paradise found.

4

The Tahoe Rim Trail

*I ascended today the highest peak near us, from which
we had a beautiful view of a mountain lake at our feet,
about fifteen miles in length, and so entirely surrounded
by mountains that we could not discover an outlet.*

—John C. Frémont, February 14, 1844

PROBABLY SHOULD SAY that I began to question my sanity for my
continued insistence on embarking on solo backpacking trips. But
I really didn't. All my solo trips up to that point had several common
themes: I get lonely. I suffer through physical pain from grueling days
of hiking and carrying too much weight. I tend to find myself in not
necessarily life-threatening but certainly interesting and challenging
predicaments. But then I would counterbalance these difficulties by
contemplating the happiness that lights up my heart when I sit alone
and listen to the gentle waves caress the shore of a mountain lake, or
watch the alpenglow slowly put the kibosh on a glorious day. I guess
I kept doing it because I believed that eventually the joys of the journey and the deep emotional satisfactions of the experience would
overwhelm that pit of darkness that I felt every evening when I faced
another night alone in my tent. Or perhaps that is all poppycock: even
given all the evidence to the contrary, I still refused to believe that I
was a wimp. I mean, people survived six months of hiking alone on
the Pacific Crest Trail, so what the hell was my problem? I just needed
to keep getting back out there and find my rhythm.

I decided that what I really needed to do was take two weeks and
hike the entire Tahoe Rim Trail (TRT). A six-day trip was just not
enough time. I needed to make it tougher. I needed to not only get
back up on the horse but make sure that it was a bucking bronco.
While perhaps crazy, I was not stupid. Hiking the Tahoe Rim Trail has
several advantages: First, it's a busy trail, with lots of people around,

so how could I be lonely? Second, lots of road crossings make it an easy trail to abandon if I had had enough, especially since it is so close to home. Third, I wrote the guidebook to the Tahoe Rim Trail. I knew the trail really well. Besides, it was time to update the guidebook, so I would have plenty to do when I sat around in camp. I wasn't just testing myself and doing something stupid, I was doing the necessary field research. Fourth, while I had hiked every inch of the trail several times, I had never thru-hiked it. Fifth, and best of all, I lived just half a mile from the trail, so I could literally walk out my door, make my way through the woods to the TRT and two weeks later stroll right back into my driveway. How cool is that?

DAY ONE

The early July day began with the Tour de France on TV. As the racers barreled across the finish line, I stood up, stretched, and smiled at what amazing athletes they are—even if some are pumped up with chemicals. I've done 100-mile days on my bike, and I was a blithering idiot, barely short of hallucinating, when I crossed the finish line, and that wasn't even a race. But these guys! They push themselves to the limits of human endurance for one hundred miles and still have enough left in the tank to sprint to the finish line. And then they do it again every day for three weeks. Finally, with a big sigh, I glanced at the clock: "Holy shit…I'm late! I was supposed to be on the trail hours ago."

First, I quickly checked my email, where I discovered that the vacation-response program that I had set up for my clients was kind enough to send thirty emails to everyone on my address list telling them that I would be gone for two weeks. "In case you didn't know, I am out of town. And if you don't believe me, read the other twenty-nine emails I am sending you." Nothing like heading into the wilderness realizing that everybody you know is either hating you for sending those confounded emails or planning to ransack your house. But eventually, all the distractions and excuses were gone. I had committed to doing this. I needed to get out of my comfy chair, put that damn pack on, and walk out the door.

Finally, I hoisted up my pack, paused at the edge of my driveway, and took that first big step into the forest. I strolled through an aspen-bordered meadow to a sparkling spring, where a narrow connector trail led to a small streamlet at the edge of Page Meadows. After exploring an oven where Basque sheepherders would bake bread when they were taking a break from carving erotic drawings in the nearby aspens, I reached the Tahoe Rim Trail. My initial reluctance to hit the trail was now supplanted by how lucky I felt to actually, finally, be embarking on this grand journey.

As I was leaving Page Meadows, I gazed past the wildflowers to the mighty visage of Twin Peaks, standing in bold relief against the crisp blue sky, a patch of snow still clinging to its north-facing slope. I then realized that if all went according to plan, two weeks later, I would top the ridge between Blackwood and Ward Canyons and look down on where I was now. Just a few more miles and I would be home. But first, I had 165 miles to walk.

A few hours later, I was at the busy 64 Acres Park in Tahoe City, sitting at a picnic table next to the Truckee River. I'd lived in Tahoe City almost all my life, so it was quite bizarre being in the most familiar of places, but instead of being on a leisurely ride with the rest of the throngs on the bike trail, I was leaning on my cumbersome pack and trying not to think about the eight miles I still had to walk that day. I was surrounded by the "I must be on vacation now" smell of suntan lotion wafting from bathing suit–clad twentysomethings trying to manage both an unwieldy raft and an ice chest full of beer. Feeling like a visitor from another planet, I snuck into the bushes, trying to hide from the horde of cheering rafters floating past, and donned a bathing suit for a swim that I reminded myself would be my last on the trail until Star Lake, almost ninety miles away. While it is nice to begin my adventure right from my house, it now seemed like bad planning to end up floating in the Truckee River on mile five. Can I take a rain check and arrange for this swim at mile forty-five please?

Too soon, it was time to leave the river's edge and begin the long climb out of Tahoe City. I tried not to dwell on the fact that Tahoe City is the lowest point on the entire TRT or that I would encounter a total of 25,000 feet of ascents and an equal amount of descents on my two-week journey. I climbed away from Lake Tahoe and wound my way north along the edge of the Truckee River Canyon. Giant sugar and Jeffrey pines held court at the top of the sunny ridgeline. Far below, rafters slowly flowed downstream. Perhaps they were the same people I saw hours earlier, only now with half as much beer in the cooler. It was a long climb, and I was feeling the distance and dreaming about jettisoning items from my pack to reduce weight. Eventually, I made it to Painted Rock, my dry campsite for the night.

I sat atop a pile of lava rock with an open view into the deep, notched Squaw Valley, which sat several thousand feet lower, yet just a few miles away as the eagle soars.

The Painted Rock viewpoint is a popular spot for mountain bikers. In fact, as I began to set up camp, three people with whom I worked pedaled up on their afternoon ride. While I was about to spend my first of thirteen nights on the trail, in less than an hour they would be in the shower and then enjoying freshly grilled steaks off the barbie with ice-cold beer. While they sat back on a soft couch and took a nap, I would be eating gooey, freeze-dried mystery food and sitting on a rock.

As a steady stream of dark clouds rolled in, threatening rain, I did my first campsite futz of the trip, flitting around to make sure everything could withstand a downpour. While I waited for the rain, I also waited for a delivery of water, since there is no water on this section of trail. My friend Kevin had agreed to ride up to Painted Rock and bring me a gallon, but as the sun tucked itself in for the night behind the mountains, I hadn't seen him yet and I started to delve into what it would mean if he didn't show up. The nearest water was six miles away, and I wouldn't be able to get there and back before dark. While at home, water is the basic ingredient that only requires an easy lift of a finger to acquire. On a backpack trip, it is the be-all and end-all, that one essential ingredient that every recipe must have.

Just about the time I began to lean solidly in the direction of a major freak-out, Kevin arrived, and I was once again reminded that while this was a solo hike, it was still totally dependent upon the kindness of friends. For example, Kevin got off work, strapped eight pounds of water on his back, and rode his bike for eight miles uphill to bring me what I needed to stay alive. He then turned around and rolled back home (where I imagined he would in less than an hour be drinking a beer and putting some tasty tidbit on the barbecue, before lying down on his comfy couch, not that I am at all bitter about that).

Refreshed and assured that I would not die of thirst, I enjoyed the evening alpenglow while contemplating my trip. I intended to revel in the beauty of the trail and appreciate in real time the incredible opportunity I have been given to be out here. As necessary, I told myself, I will return to the peacefulness and meditation that can be found by just focusing on putting one foot in front of the other. Repeat if necessary. I reminded myself of the advantages of being alone: I can go my own speed, not waiting for someone slower or hiking faster than

I want to keep up. I can totally control when I start hiking, when I stop, and when I finish for the day. I can eat when and what I want. But as I have seen on past trips, when I'm by myself, I don't always control my mind. Sometimes, it likes to go into dark, lonely places and I have to keep yanking it back out into the light of day (which can be a challenge because it usually goes into those places when I am in my tent in the dark).

Perhaps the problem with loneliness is that our culture has instilled this image of the lonely person as a loser. Some sort of mentally defective individual who is either wiling away the days slurping chicken soup while sadly doing nothing in their squalid apartment, or much worse, is planning some horrible crime against all the folks whom they blame for their loneliness. Inevitably when there is a TV story about a recent mass murder, someone with a camera in their face proclaims, "Oh, he was a loner, didn't see him much, he was quiet and kept to himself."

So when a guy like myself who is basically happy, has good social connections, and is satisfied with my accomplishments feels lonely and sad in a tent in the wilderness, I begin to wonder what is my problem. Am I on my way to the land of chicken soup? Or is loneliness just the universal condition that no one talks about, but everyone lives with in their own private way? We all just buck up, find something to keep us busy, and try to forget about that empty feeling. Those pangs of loneliness hit us in the gut while we are lying in the tent because we feel vulnerable to whatever monsters are creeping around out there. Or maybe since in the still quiet of night there are no distractions, our minds can focus on how in life we truly are alone.

DAY TWO

At four o'clock in the afternoon, the traffic roared by on busy Highway 267 near the top of Brockway Summit as I sat on a log just above the road, baking in the hot afternoon sun. After twelve miles of dusty walking, I was ready to lay my head down, but instead I was once again anxiously anticipating a friend delivering eight pounds of water that would keep me alive. And force me to remove my ass from this log to start hiking again.

It was just the second day, and the stifling heat had already given me a shining red blister with an exclamation mark on each little toe as well as another on the side of my right foot. That one had a translucent puffy sac of fluid just waiting to be popped. If muscle straining, food depravation, and the lack of a shower are not enough to put things in perspective…just mix in blisters for that certain extra painful touch to the hiking experience. With a blister, that painful touch comes with every step. A long backpacking trip is somewhat like one of those Tough Mudder obstacle course challenges. Let's listen to the trailer for the Tahoe Rim Trail Mudder…

"That's right, Johnny, our contestants will begin their challenge by putting on a 30-pound pack which they will then drag up and over mountains for fourteen straight days. Now, while that's more than many can handle, we like to make things even more interesting by adding a series of painful obstacles for our contestants to face along the way. Every day, they must confront the Fake Food Challenge. From the second day on, with every step, they have to get through the truly painful Blister Boil. And of course, there's the always-entertaining I Can't Find Enough Water Contest. By Day Four, they are confronting the Stench Slide. For the pièce de résistance, every night they have to get through seven hours of what for many is the most difficult challenge of all: Alone in your Tent in the Dark."

■ ■ ■

Making the journey in one continuous walk, instead of heading out for a day and then returning home at night, seemed to make the lake that much more sparkling blue, the greenery more vibrantly green. I felt much more connected to the trail when every step was part of the process of completing this grand circle of the lake. Every step one step farther from the start, one step closer to the conclusion.

Since I was hiking at the peak of the tourist season, however, there was no doubting the popularity of Lake Tahoe. On the distant surface of the lake, miniature boats rushed in all directions, leaving dozens of crisscrossed shimmering lines. I wasn't sure where they were going, but they were in a hurry to get there. Any time I was within a few miles of a road, I could hear the constant drone of cars, which I'm sure were filled with tourists scurrying to get to the lake so they could spend hours doing nothing on the beach.

My friend eventually arrived with life-sustaining waters, and I slogged my tired ass off the log and up the steep, powdery trail to the Flintstone viewpoint. Water might sustain life, but adding eight pounds to your pack at the end of a hot day just amplifies that extra level of torture. But as a San Francisco Giants fan, I know that sometimes the seemingly never-ending torture is rewarded with something spectacular in the end.

Flintstone Rocks, while not quite as exciting as the Giants finally winning the World Series in 2010, was a worthwhile reward. The lake spread out magnificently to the south, and as I scrunched my tiny tent into a minuscule nook between flat piles of cartoonish rocks, the sun was dropping into the mountains, and I was quite pleased to discover that it would be an enchanting spot to take in the sunset. Soon, a steady stream of folks clambered up the rocks to join me in the sunset celebration. We talked briefly and mundanely, and then just as it was getting dark, they all walked back to their homes nearby, leaving me alone. Yeah, yeah, I know, I know, you don't have to remind me, they were taking showers, putting meat on the barbie and quaffing a cold one.

Hiking the Tahoe Rim Trail was like going to the eighth-grade dance. There were all these people around to talk to, and then when the dance was over, everybody cleared out and you had to go home by yourself. Actually in life, we are alone as well: we just make a lot of effort to deceive ourselves that we are not. We work hard to be surrounded by spouses, kids, siblings, parents or coworkers. But in the dark of night, alone in a tent, we face the reality that we make our own decisions and we have to live with them. It was reassuring in some ways on the Tahoe Rim Trail that you could hear the dogs barking and kids screaming from all those homes not too far away, but it also reinforced that out there, it was just me.

This trip, so close to home yet so far away, was a vacation from reality while staying in the same place. The weirdness of seeing my backyard but not being able to touch it was highlighted when I had those brief contacts with friends, who then headed back to their normal lives. It's as if I have stepped into some sort of weird space-time continuum where for two weeks I was watching my world from above. It looked the same as it always does, but for now, I was not a part of it.

DAY THREE

I just couldn't take my eyes off the incredible pinks, oranges, and purples of the slow-motion sunset, and then, a few hours later, the earth and sky were back at it again, dishing out another feast of pinks emerging from the gray. A chance for gratitude. While those day hikers last night had to hightail it back home before the show was over to beat the darkness, I got to watch the sunset unfolding before me. When we are home, we could find a lovely place to watch the day end, but we usually don't. If the sky is alight with color, we might glimpse it between dinner and another session of screen staring. In the wilderness, away from the distractions of humanity, the sunset is the evening show, and there is only one channel to watch. After the sunset, the next show begins, the infinite story of the stars.

Day Three was a transition day. I climbed away from the stately Jeffrey pines and thick clumps of white firs into the western white pines with their long, narrow cones, the mountain hemlocks covered from foot to head in the darkest of green needles, and the red-barked ancient juniper that spend centuries tucked into rocky cliffs hiding their blue gin berries. I left the trees of civilization, the weedy firs and pines that Tahoe folks find fenced in their backyards, and climbed to where the wild trees are. Trees beaten and twisted by the ferocious winter storms. It takes a commitment to reach these trees. You must climb for miles to feel the shade of a hemlock or white pine.

At one rocky point on the ridge, just above a grove of twisted ancient hemlocks, I stood and slowly spun around. To the south lay a long, gentle sweep of green forest, sweeping into Kings Beach, hugging the edge of the twenty-mile bowl of blue, Lake Tahoe. To the west, brown stripes of the Northstar ski runs slashed through the trees down the face of Mount Pluto. Farther out, a quick ribbon of dark blue, Donner Lake, and above that, a knob of volcanic rock standing guard above the crest of the Sierra, Castle Peak atop Donner Pass. To the north, three more patches of blue, the human-made mega bathtubs: Prosser, Boca, and Stampede Reservoirs. It's a view that captures a mish-mash of civilization and bands of wildness: life in the Tahoe Sierra.

I was feeling stronger. Zaps of pain from my blisters still sparked, but I was beginning to find my mojo. Like the trees, I was transitioning into the wilder pattern of life on the trail. A longer backpacking trip is all about getting into a routine and finding meditation while you walk the miles. It didn't hurt that this day dished out mile after gorgeous mile of seemingly endless fields of mule ears in the foreground with the dark-blue waters of Tahoe dominating the background. As is often the case on the Tahoe Rim Trail, I spent the day confronting the oxymoron of this hike: you walk for miles gazing at this huge, delicious body of cool, blue water, and yet there is no water anywhere near you to drink. The answer to that conundrum might be found in the name of the trail. It often follows the rim or crest of the mountains around Lake Tahoe, and I think I read somewhere that water flows downhill and away from the highest point.

The most remarkable thing about the Tahoe Rim Trail is that much of the time you have the opportunity to gauge where you have gone, and where you have yet to go. Looking across the lake, you can see your future. From the pile of rocks through which the trail winds on the southern slope of Rose Knob Peak, I looked south to Freel Peak, which stood out as a rounded, treeless summit standing high above the far distant southern shore. In a few long days of hiking, I would look back from that saddle toward Rose Knob Peak and see where I was. For me, ever since I took a good gander at Twin Peaks from my start at Page Meadows, it had been my point of orientation. Even though I'd been hiking for just a few days, Twin Peaks was already reduced from a monstrous presence dominating the skyline to a mere blip on the top of a ridge in the distance. As I slogged my way through the miles, it felt as if they were adding up oh so slowly, but then when I saw how much smaller Twin Peaks had become in just a few days, I was impressed with what a hiking stud I was after all.

Tahoe day hikers fall into three groups. The first are experienced hikers. They are wearing synthetic clothing that wicks away moisture, and they are carrying plenty of food and water, a first aid kit, and an extra layer of clothing. They know where they are going, how much elevation gain is involved, and how long it will take to get there. While these folks will never need to be rescued because of ineptitude, you may get a headache from rolling your eyes after listening to their pompous droning on about the latest two-hundred-dollar titanium hiking gadget that shaved a quarter ounce off their pack weight.

The second are Lake Tahoe Bucket Listers. They clearly saw a notation on the list of things to do when they visit Lake Tahoe that says: "Take a hike." It doesn't matter too much what they are wearing or what they brought or failed to bring with them on the trail because they only have an hour allotted on their schedule for a hike. Fueled by seven cups of coffee from Fire Sign Cafe, they make a mad dash to a lovely view of Tahoe that they saw on Instagram, take ten quick photos to post on Facebook, and are off to the next item on their list, a cruise on the *Tahoe Gal,* which they hoped would return to the dock just in time for their spa appointment, followed by a dinner reservation.

Then there is the group of "hikers" whom I find most fascinating. You meet them at four o'clock in the afternoon as they are on their way into the wilderness and you are rushing to get out before dark. Usually it's a couple, and you can tell immediately that one thought this was a great idea and the other would rather be held down on the ground and repeatedly bludgeoned with a sledgehammer. They are dressed in beat-up, old tennis shoes with holes in them that appear to have been dragged from under the back seat of their car. They are wearing cotton sweatpants or thin cotton shorts and a cotton T-shirt, which is drenched with sweat. They are sharing one tiny, down-to-the-last-dregs water bottle. With dazed looks in their eyes, gasping for breath, and a desperate voice that is between pleading and whining, they ask, "How far is it to the lake?"

You are not sure which lake they are seeking, since they are on a trail with a few, but that's OK, because they don't know the name of the lake either. What you do know is that the closest lake is at least five miles farther with about 1,500 feet of climbing, and there is no way in hell they are going to make it and get back out before dark. I always try to stop and give them a few bits of helpful information, like how's about bringing along some water next time and then of course the really cogent advice…turn around now, while you still have a chance. It's amazing more people don't die in the woods.

■ ■ ■

At the end of the day, I reached Gray Lake, the first water source on this section of trail. Gray Creek begins as a spring, popping up from the immense talus field holding on to the steep north slope of Rose Knob Peak. It travels just one hundred feet, before gurgling past a garden of yellow buttercups into tiny Gray Lake. This lake is a clear example of the first rule of water body–naming in the United States: the less water that is available in a region, the more emphasis is given to any body of water that appears. Easterners look at what those of us in the arid West proudly call a river and say that's just a dang creek (in some places pronounced "crick," followed by a spit of tobacco). A little pond like Gray Lake, which is really just a pool in a small creek, would remain unnamed in most parts of the country. Here it gets glorified with the title "Lake" because it sits more than ten miles from the nearest substantial body of water.

Although it's small, Gray Lake is appealing. After a brief but spectacular foray through a prolific display of wildflowers, the bustling creek briefly widens and stills, becoming tiny Gray Lake for about one hundred yards, before trickling out the other side through a wake of yellow monkey flowers. Then just a bit past its outlet, the creek rages down a steep slope surrounded by a deep forest and disappears into the wide expanse of the Mount Rose Wilderness.

Since it had been a few days since I had immersed myself, Gray Lake's clear, fresh water looked enticing. I got about ten feet into the lake and then began sinking a foot or more into the gooey, gray mud… soft, yes; sandy, no. It felt quite nice on my aching feet though, like a cold-water mud bath. But now my formerly crystal-clear lake was a mess of light-gray, whirling mire. When I attempted to remove my feet from the ooze, it refused to relinquish. Loud glooping noises accompanied each time I wrenched my tootsies clear and took another step to escape the muck. Eventually, I made it to the grassy edge, rinsed off the gray chalk, and settled into one of the nicest campsites on the Tahoe Rim Trail.

It was a large, flat expanse, close to the rustling creek, with a few ancient pines providing bits of shady escape from the heat. Several downed dead trees, barkless and bleached white, served as tables for my laundry to dry. I set up the solar charger, checked on the laundry every few minutes, wrote and read and whiled away a few hours of the late afternoon. Even though I was only about ten miles from a major road, the huge mass of Rose Knob Peak was between Gray Lake and Lake Tahoe, blocking all signs of humanity.

Once again, and certainly not for the last time, I confronted the lonely solo hikers' afternoon challenge: your camp is fully set up, there is nothing on your agenda that has to be completed, so now what do you do? When you are with someone else, this is the relaxing and recuperating part of the trip. A time for talking about the important things that are going on in your life, or perhaps nothing at all, but someone is there as a sounding board if needed. For the lone hiker, however, it is the time when you have to fight to keep boredom from sneaking over to the dark side and becoming a case of the dreaded I'm Lonely, Poor, Poor, Pitiful Me Syndrome. That's when some folks pick up a fishing pole or a book so they are doing something to occupy the brain. Whether fishing actually occupies your brain is debatable. (Don't get all riled up now, fisher people or whatever the heck the term is nowadays; just trying to see if you are paying attention.)

The more you hike by yourself, the more you understand why long-distance thru-hikers keep marching on and compiling enormous distances. They can't really face all that down time alone with their thoughts. So they keep walking, only stopping to eat and sleep. They get really strong so they can keep hiking. They are obsessed with the 2,000 miles they still have to hike before the snow flies, so they keep hiking. They get bored and lonely if they stop, so they keep hiking.

In 2011, Scott Williamson, who lived near Lake Tahoe in Truckee, California, broke his own record for solo hiking the Pacific Crest Trail by traversing more than 2,600 miles in just sixty-four days. That's right, all you junior mathematicians, that's almost forty-one per day (and that's not counting all the extra miles he walked to go off the trail for resupplies). While hiking forty-one miles in one day would be an incredible challenge, I can imagine doing it (although my daily record is twenty-six miles). What I cannot imagine is getting up the next morning and tromping off another forty-one miles. It would be a struggle just dragging my very sorry, oh, my God, I can't believe I hiked forty-one miles yesterday, ass out of my sleeping bag. Hiking another forty-one miles would be out of the question. And don't forget these Pacific Crest Trail miles are at high elevation with hefty climbs and steep descents—not like walking on a bike trail along the edge of the ocean. Sometimes it seems like there is no limit to what some humans can do. Not me, mind you, but some humans.

Scott told me that he would get up at five o'clock in the morning and as quickly as possible start walking, then hike until dark. Sometimes he would fall asleep while hiking and when he hit the ground he would startle awake, get up, and start hiking again. Since he has hiked the PCT a number of times, including several yo-yos (in which you walk from Mexico to Canada, stop for a quick stretch, then turn around and hike back), he probably could hike it sleeping. He doesn't want to sleep through it though. He does it because he loves every inch of the trail and is fascinated to see how it looks different this time than all the other times he has hiked it. I wonder, not that it would ever happen, but what if he were to set up camp at three o'clock in the afternoon? Would he spend the few hours before dark in quiet meditation, or go completely bonkers? I'm thinking he would hang out for about a half hour, say "Screw this," and put in another ten or fifteen miles before bed.

As I sat there alone at Gray Lake, I began wondering if you get even more bored after spending weeks and weeks of alone time. What more could you possibly have to say to yourself? You spend half your time enjoying the breathtaking views, but during the other half you have already analyzed to death what you should do about your jobs, relationships, kids, money, what would make you happy, blah, blah, blah…and on and on. Enough already. You are still on the trail, and you are not going to change anything until you get back. So you obsess about pizza or that great song that you can't get out of your head, or a cool glass of lemonade, or ice tea, or an ice cream cone. It all just swirls around in your brain telling you over and over again, "When I get there, I'm going to do this, and, boy, is it going to be fun."

A few years ago, I was hiking a portion of the TRT that was also a portion of the Pacific Crest Trail and chatted with a few thru-hikers. If you want a truly interesting conversation, it's always great to talk to somebody who has been hiking for one thousand miles straight through desert, snowy passes, multiple bear encounters, and a cornucopia of colorful blisters that made most of the two-and-a-half-million steps it took to get here painful ones. Look into these gallant hikers' eyes and you will a see steely determination that cries out, "I will finish this damn trail no matter what it takes." But you will also see a vacant, distant stare, like the look Grandpa gives when he tells tales of the battle he barely survived in Korea.

It is important to wait to have a lengthy conversation with a thru-hiker until you have spent at least a few days in the woods yourself… long enough to build up your own stench to slightly offset the powerful bouquet coming from the guy or gal who hasn't had a shower in weeks. Aside from the stench, you are not really residing on the same planet as these guys until you have hiked a number of days and confronted the reality of long-distance hiking.

■ ■ ■

While the PCT thru-hikers are probably ticking off another ten miles, I sit alone with my thoughts, and lots of them, along the shores of Gray Lake. I marveled at the enormous lodgepole pines, which have found this isolated, high-altitude freeze zone as the perfect place to hang their hat for a few hundred years. The lodgepole spends its youth packed tightly together with all the other little lodgepoles that look just like it: dull gray, narrow-trunked, spindly, and not really attracting much attention. Tree weeds like those dang ubiquitous white firs that flow over the Sierra landscape. A few rare and lucky specimens, however, somehow avoid the beetle, drought, and fire, and keep growing, eventually outlasting their lodgepole compatriots and finding their perfect niche. When they live a few hundred years, they grow wide and robust, with thick, soft-red bark trunks reaching high into the sky and stout branches flailing out in every direction. Also near Gray Lake, tucked against the north-facing slope of Rose Knob Peak, sits a massive grove of mountain hemlocks. They're packed in like sardines, loaded with diminutive cones with a delicate, complicated texture. If you see a lot of hemlocks, consider it fair warning that this place gets a lot of snow: hemlocks are total powder hounds. They love the deep stuff. That's why they hang out at ski areas.

While I have always marveled at the beauty of trees, it was when I delved more deeply into their startling complexity that I began to realize they have been the superheroes of plant life for more than four hundred million years. What drove this incredible period of longevity is the remarkable substance we call wood. According to Hope Jahren in her book, *Lab Girl*, wood is not only as strong as iron, but more flexible and lighter weight. Wood is so sturdy it enables trees to stand incredibly tall and hold possession of a precious bit of real estate for hundreds of years. Wood is also porous, allowing the tree to carry copious quantities of precious water all the way from the deep recesses of the soil to the tippy top of the tree.

The conifers that have adapted to live in a cold climate can survive standing in below-freezing temperatures for a good chunk of the year. Not a big deal? Go stand naked in the middle of February with no food or water when the temperature is twenty-two degrees and the wind is blowing at twenty-five miles an hour and see how long you would last. A day maybe, and not a happy one. Trees, though, create their own natural antifreeze. Each fall they go through a hardening process, which removes water from wood cells and instead concentrates proteins, sugars, and acid in a slurry. They begin this process not because of dropping temperatures, but via their ability to calculate that the length of days is getting shorter, and then amazingly, what day is just the right time to act. If they begin the process too soon, they lose precious growing time. If they start too late, they may freeze.

Another amazing factor behind the long-term survival of trees is their ability to adapt to attacks from their biggest enemy: insects. Jahren tells a story of trees that were attacked by caterpillars. The caterpillars won the first battle, removing a hefty supply of the trees' leaves, but then the trees, like the Ents in *The Lord of the Rings*, fought back and began to flood the leaves with a form of caterpillar poison. The fight against the caterpillars also triggered a production of Volatile Organic Compounds, or VOCs. Waves of VOCs can travel through the air up to a mile and when they reach other trees in the hood, they alert them to begin producing the stuff that the caterpillars don't like. By the time those pesky crawlers reach those other trees, it's too late for them to do any damage. While trees may not have brains, they communicate with each other in slow motion, perhaps more effectively than those of us who supposedly have brains.

Once I'd exhausted my religious devotion to the lodgepoles and the hemlocks, I returned to the art of camp futzing. Move the solar charger. Eat. Clean the dishes and set them out to dry. Brush teeth. Put away the bear canister. Write. Remember I forgot to put something in the bear canister, go get it and try again. Wander around thinking about what to do next. Go to the bathroom, which of course is a misnomer, since there is no bathroom. Wash hands. Filter water. Soak blisters in the cold water. Get hungry again. Tell myself not to eat. Say "Screw it," eat. Brush teeth again. Put away bear canister again. Look around wondering what to do next. Sit in tent, write. Sit outside, write. Walk over to the lake to look at flowers and trees. Read. Get back in tent. Check time and realize I still have two more interminable hours until it gets dark. I knew there was a reason I liked hiking in October when the days were shorter, and as soon as your body was exhausted from the hiking, you could immediately start getting ready to head to sleep.

At eight in the evening, the last rays lit up the rocky pile of talus bright rose at the base of Rose Knob Peak. The only sounds were the soft rush of wind rustling through the ancient lodgepoles, the gentle rolling gurgle of the creek, and the high-pitched whistling of birds, singing goodnight.

DAY FOUR

In the middle of the night, unmarred by artificial light, the sky was an endless sea of black—the stars popping out of the darkness like snow-flakes. I wanted to continue viewing this seemingly endless pano-rama of stars all night long, but I realized: at 9,000 feet in this deep bowl at two in the morning, it was freaking cold. So I put it back in my pants and dove back into my sleeping bag. One of the facts about sleeping outside on cold nights is that you often only find yourself appreciating the lovely sky while taking a pee break. An advantage of getting older is that a smaller bladder provides more opportuni-ties to ponder the universe.

A few hours later, it was even colder as I numb-fingered my way about camp, trying to rub up enough heat to get my mind off my frozen hands. When you are on a leisurely hike with friends, a brutally cold morning will leave you emerging from the sleeping bag late for a bit of nice conversation over coffee or cocoa while the sun slowly gets around to providing the warmth that you crave. When you're alone and on a time schedule, however, the only thing to be done about it is to get off your butt and start hiking.

Leaving Gray Lake, I soon forgot about cold fingers and toes and began to concentrate more on somehow bringing enough of that cold, thin air into my lungs to slog up the steep hill. One of the great methods of eliminating one type of pain is to create a different pain somewhere else. By the time I'd huffed my way to the saddle above Mud Lake, I'd burned some warmth into my limbs and was ready for a well-deserved break. There before me was Mud Lake, a poor excuse for a spot to contemplate. It is aptly named since even in the wettest years, all that the lake reviewers Eskel and Siebert could say about it is, "Well, it's not as nice as Gray, but I guess it's water." After a dry winter, however, the reviewers would only say that it's "a mud hole that isn't worth my time."

Once past Mud, the next stage of the route winds past craggy, red, volcanic knobs, smooth granite slabs and up, up, up to the top of Relay Peak, at 10,300 feet, the highest point on the TRT. It began with the big blue beautifulness of Lake Tahoe dominating the view to the south, and at my feet, the delicate, luscious, yellow, and red goodness that are the woody-fruited evening primroses—a flower that only deigns itself to grow in the vicinity of Mount Rose.

As I was puffing my way toward the top, hands on knees, staring at the ground, while trying to remind myself that eventually this infernal uphill would end, I ran into my super-fit friend Joe. Well, actually, he ran into me. He was taking what for him was a pleasant morning run on the entire twenty-mile section between Brockway Summit and Tahoe Meadows with its 3,000 feet of elevation gain. He had already flown through about fifteen tough miles by the time I saw him. Why did he still look perfectly refreshed? He was just another reminder of the universal truth of all athletic endeavors: You will always be surrounded by people who are much more fit than you. And then those people, with whom you are so impressed because they can kick your ass, will get left in the dust by another person who has attained an even higher level of human fitness. Joe, for example, has completed several Ironman competitions. To me, doing a 2.5-mile swim, 112-mile bike ride, and a 26.2-mile run in about fifteen hours is an inspiring, but impossible endeavor. But take those Ironman competitors and tell them they have to pull a Scott Williamson, walking forty-one miles a day for sixty-four straight days, and they would have to bow to Scott and say, "You win."

I did eventually reach the top, where the treeless north-facing bowl drops precipitously down to a rock pile, then a wave of forest and deep canyons descend even farther into the heart of the Mount Rose Wilderness. In the far distance, Interstate 80 slices through the Truckee River canyon. Often while driving I-80 to Reno, I'd looked up to this distant ridge, the farthest and highest mountain in view, to catch a glimpse of a little blip of a relay tower, which now sat in bold relief just a half mile down the ridge.

To the south, the vast green flat of Tahoe Meadows flowed into dark forest, my next major goal. I made the illogical logical decision that since this was the highest point on the trail, it must be all downhill from here, so I hung around and socialized with the steady stream of peak baggers who were pretty dang excited to see me.... I'm sure that was it; it wasn't that I was sitting in front of the canister where they could sign in as having reached the high point on the TRT.

■   ■   ■

Soon enough, I confronted the yin and yang that dominates my solo hiking experience: When I spend long periods alone on the trail, I get lonely. But once I start seeing too many people, I quickly begin to plan my exit strategy to return to my protective cocoon of silence.

These phenomena only occur when I'm backpacking solo. When I am out hiking with friends or guiding a hiking trip, I enjoy the camaraderie of conversation or the opportunity to introduce newcomers to the joys of the trail. But when I am alone, I suffer from lonely hiker syndrome. Perhaps they will come up with a cure just like they did for restless legs syndrome. Unfortunately, one of the drugs taken to cure RLS has a few pesky side effects, including addiction to gambling and sex. That's OK; I think I will work on a solution without the drugs.

With just four miles of downhill to go to reach the Mount Rose TRT Trailhead on Highway 431, I braced myself for the massive throng of humans I was about to encounter. The Mount Rose Trailhead is the closest TRT access to Reno, which gives the crowd of short-distance hikers a view-filled two-and-a-half-mile stroll up to beautiful Galena Falls. It has become the most popular stretch on the entire Tahoe Rim Trail. Head down, I quickly scampered through the swarms of flip-flopping, non-water-carrying amblers peeping at the waterfall and made my way to the crossing of Highway 431. Phew, now with the hordes behind me, it was just an easy mile stroll through lush meadows dotted with purple Elephant heads to the Tahoe Meadows trailhead.

There at the trailhead, under a pop-up tent sat an active aid station for the Tahoe Rim Trail Endurance Runs (one hundred miles, fifty miles, and fifty-five kilometers), which was in mid-stride. I plopped into a chair designed for the real athletes and started chatting with the friendly volunteer at the post. Apparently, I looked like I had hiked four hundred miles instead of forty because she quickly began dishing out wonderfulness. She offered me an icy bit of grape popsicle goodness, followed by a warm, chewy, melt-in-your-mouth cookie entrée and a bottle of cold water. Then she graced me with the most valuable award of all, an official race hat, which I promptly donned, adopting its slogan as my motto for the rest of the trip: "A glimpse of heaven, a taste of hell."

While I was basking in the glow of all this largesse, a young lady who was thru-hiking the trail in just eight days stopped into the aid station. She started in Tahoe City as well, but she made it to Gray Lake in one day (apparently, I didn't have the lake to myself the night before after all) as opposed to what she must consider my leisurely three days. Listening to this woman's plans for another ten more miles today made me want to hike longer as well...tomorrow. I didn't know whether to congratulate her on her strength and courage or introduce her to Scott Williamson to put everything in perspective. You did 165 miles in eight days? Oh, really? Scott could hike it in four. By the way, the record for running the entire Tahoe Rim Trail at the time I was writing this was thirty-nine hours, and that was by a guy who got lost for a few miles in the middle of the night. Like I've been saying, there is no limit to the power of human endurance...just not every human's endurance.

Then of course non–record breakers counter with the attitude: "Don't forget to stop and smell the flowers." Yeah, well, to do that, you have to take your pack off and then get it back on, so unless those flowers are as tall as I and smell really good I will just appreciate their beauty as I walk by. Or the other suggestion with which I do agree: "Stop and go for a swim." I'm all for that, but the TRT does not provide many of those opportunities. On the TRT, the water you see is exquisitely beautiful, but only to be looked at from a distance, not to be touched. Apparently, Lake Tahoe is a supermodel.

■ ■ ■

I ambled across Tahoe Meadows and found a campsite in the trees, about one hundred yards off the trail, just a short walk from Ophir Creek. At first blush, it seemed like a lovely site: far enough away from Highway 431 that noise shouldn't be a problem, yet close enough to Ophir Creek that water was available for drinking and hopefully a desperately needed removal of the dried-on remains of my foray into the Gray Lake mud pits the night before.

As it meanders through the meadow, Ophir Creek is cool and clear but very narrow and in most places barely visible behind a thick wall of scratchy brush. I delicately scraped and sardined myself into a one-foot-deep, six-inch-wide pool of gently flowing water. Once I was mostly wet, I took a deep breath and surveyed the dozens of scratches up and down my arms and legs, and I realized that I could hardly move without exfoliating another painful layer on this willow pitchfork. The water was frigid, though, so I didn't have a lot of time to analyze solutions. I kept my arms and legs in tight, spun around in little circles in the water, like I was being wrapped up in a blanket trying to put out a fire. As I exited, I scraped off one more layer of skin then stumbled my way back to my campsite.

DAY FIVE

It's a good thing that nice volunteer gave me food and a hat yesterday, because all night long I was not happy with those races. While I was one hundred yards away from the trail, that was not nearly far enough since the really long-distance runners go all night and have spotters. These spotters, whose necks I gleefully imagined wringing, spent the night running with and attempting to encourage the semi-comatose race participants. Throughout the night, I was treated to: "YEAH, YOU CAN DO IT...JUST A LITTLE HILL UP AHEAD... KEEP GOING!" One little pod after another of perky cheerleaders were trying to rah-rah their dispirited zombies up the hill.

During a brief break from the motivational speakers, I was drifting off to sleep when I was startled awake with a teeth-chattering "BRUMMMMMFFFFF...BRUMMMMMFFFFF." A short time later, I heard it again.

"Brummmmmfffff...Brummmmmfffff..." Eventually, the dim light bulb in my brain turned on. It was the rumble strips designed to warn inattentive motorists who are drifting off Highway 431. While the purpose of these strips is to wake up drivers, they also serve the purpose of waking up campers a half mile away. I screamed, "Can't anyone keep a damn car on the road?" I'm certain the drivers couldn't hear me, but perhaps runners were startled out of their midnight stupor by my angry ramblings.

Just when I was at my wits' end with the sounds of the road, screaming obscenities, and the confounded chaser chorus, a generator roared to life at six bloody o'clock in the morning at that food station that twelve hours earlier was my savior. When I set up camp, I thought it was a mile away, but now it sounded like the generator was in one of those mega RVs two sites over in a crowded campground. The generator powered a bright light that looked like it was designed for interrogation. I pictured a man with a mustache smoking a cigarette while grilling me with questions, "and tell me about that time you attempted to kill a spotter?" A short time later, a faint whiff of pancakes wafted across the meadow. I waited, but no one came to my tent and took my order for a short stack with maple syrup, strawberries, and a healthy dollop of whipped cream.

To hell with sleep. At the first hint of light, I dragged myself out of the tent and slowly stumbled my way to the highway to wait for my friend Jan, who was set to meet me with an early-morning food drop.

In my dazed continence at seven in the morning, I passed a few one-hundred-mile racers. I amiably called out, "Hi, you got this," because I had the cheer down, but the mad shufflers just mumbled incoherently and kept stumbling down the trail. They paid to put themselves through this, and they still had another twenty miles to go.

Then Jan and my friend Sara, who coincidentally showed up at the trail for a run at the same time Jan arrived, walked with me. They got in a few, "Um-hummms" and "Oh, reallys?" between my endless bantering. Fortunately for them, my ceaseless chatter was interrupted about once a minute when we had to step off the trail to let another of the throng of mountain bikers pass.

■ ■ ■

Stupid Tim Trick: How does the guy who wrote the guidebook to the Tahoe Rim Trail, who is well aware that this most popular mountain biking segment on the whole TRT only allows riders on even days of the month, end up here on an even weekend day in the middle of the summer? I believe Forrest Gump had something cogent to say about that.

■ ■ ■

Eventually my jaw wore out, and I stopped babbling as we reached the long spine of the Carson Range that truly is the Tahoe Rim, the rounded ridgeline between the High Sierra and the vast expanse of Nevada desert. Far below to the east was a green patchwork of rangeland and shimmering, brownish-blue Washoe Lake, tucked up tight against the mountains. It was the first basin of the immense series of alternating basins and ranges that reaches all the way across Nevada. The mountain ranges are oriented north-south, like ships floating on the sea, while sagebrush-dotted basins fill in the gaps between those high ranges. It's a land of dry lakes, rocky crags, and wide expanses of spectacular high-desert nothingness. All these basins and ranges are part of the Great Basin, a huge area that includes almost all of Nevada where none of the water that hits the ground reaches the sea.

To the south and west of the TRT, big swaths of Lake Tahoe reach out to the Sierra Crest: a four-hundred-mile-long mountain range of granite peaks, rich forests, and mega snows that was the bane of nineteenth-century immigrants heading to California.

The trail wandered back and forth from the long-needled Jeffrey pine-dominated Tahoe side to the red firs of the eastern side whose dark-green needles shade the trail. We passed just east of the tippy top of Diamond Peak Ski Resort, then rolled along the sandy crest to reach the lower of the Twin Lakes for lunch. The lake was bone dry, but as we chewed we imagined water into existence. Sara had already run home miles earlier, but Jan was now faced with a return to the trailhead and what would turn out to be an eighteen-mile day, probably wondering a good portion of the way back why in the hell she hadn't turned around sooner.

Leaving Twin Lakes, I was once again solo guy, making my way around the Tahoe Rim Trail. The trail began the first extended climb of the day, winding up through shiny, white granite boulders on what felt like an endless series of steep, sandy switchbacks. About a mile up, while catching my breath and becoming aware that it was getting pretty damn hot, I noticed far below bluish-green water shimmering in the sunshine: Upper Twin Lake. Not visible from my lunch spot at Lower Twin Lake, all that shiny wetness now looked pretty enticing for a swim. Instead, I continued the long trudge, with still another one-and-a-half miles of climbing to go. What kept me going were frequent jumps off the trail, as another mountain biker roared through the sharp turns with a big smile on her face. Finally, the trail leveled out and reached the Christopher's Loop trail. Here a one-mile view loop leads to a spectacular vista high above Sand Harbor. Almost the entire lake unfolds below in what I feel is the best view on the entire Tahoe Rim Trail. That day, however, I slogged right by it; there was no more climbing left in these legs, and they were hell-bent for camp.

I trooped past a forest of hemlocks to a wildflower-dotted ridge top, with Marlette Lake below; in the distance was the rounded, treeless Snow Valley Peak. Then finally, in a shady forest, I reached Marlette Campground. It had a few of the basic comforts of home: a toilet, water, picnic tables, and about a half dozen tent sites sprinkled among the trees. A six-inch layer of fine, powdery, milk-chocolaty dust covered everything. And buzzing around my face, flies. Persistent, we will never give up, so you might as well give up, flies.

Ah, the tent. It truly is the refuge of the lonely hiker. You can lie down on something softer than dirt or rock, and rest your back and legs. Perhaps most importantly on this day, it was an escape from the impending insanity that was to come if I remained alone with the bugs. Many of the ultra-lightweight hikers skip the tent and go for a tarp or some other insubstantial device just in case it rains. But to me, when you are backpacking, the tent is much more than just a way to stay out of the rain. It is home. A tiny bit of personal space. A place where I can put my stuff and feel like it is in my possession. Perhaps if you hike all day and never really spend any time in camp, you can get away without a tent, but I value my personal cocoon even if it is a purely superficial separation between me and the world. Especially when that world is composed of large quantities of mosquitoes and flies.

My food drop included a book, so I cuddled with myself in the tent and read. But even after spending a good portion of the day having conversations with friends, this big camp, which could comfortably hold twenty people, was a lonely place to be by yourself. As the sun dropped behind Marlette Peak, a few riders shot by on the trail above, and I longed to have them come down to camp and say hello, but I was alone.

I pondered this trail, which has been such an important part of my life. I love her and appreciate her wily charms. But by midsummer, she is a dusty, arid bugger that creates a challenging journey. My mental stroll through the minor failings of what really is a show-stopping beauty of a pathway were interrupted in the thick forest of red firs by the constant cacophony: squirrels chirping, woodpeckers pecking, and blue jays squawking. I thought longingly of the next day when I would escape this dust bowl and dive into the cool, clear waters of Marlette Lake.

As I lay in my tent, I thought that the greatest lesson that I could have learned from the trip was the one with which I continued to struggle: how to do nothing and like it. We spend our lives rushing to fill up every moment with what we consider important, essential stuff. We focus on how to continually improve our time management. On developing the skills to make every moment count, and thus increase our productivity. Then we go backpacking and end up with a lot of time when the best thing to be doing is absolutely nothing, and it can be a challenging adjustment. Even with lots of practice, I still didn't have a clue how to do that. Of course, what I really should have been doing was writing. I mean, what better place to write than alone in a tent? But there are no limits to what a writer will do to keep from writing. We love that inner voice that keeps reminding

us to write, but we also just want to smack it across the mouth some
times, because writing is so damn hard. When we sit at home looking
at our computer trying to throw down a few choice words that connect beautifully like a river, we invent squirrel distraction techniques
that will allow us to either get up from the chair or focus on something aside from that next sentence. There in my tent, real squirrels
were there to distract me.

DAY SIX

There is certainly something to be said for a place to go No. 2 with
a view. Given my druthers, I prefer a location near a smooth rock,
where you can watch the sun move across the distant lakeshore.
Hopefully, the prime location also allots privacy so that unsuspect-
ing campers will not stumble upon your naked ass mid-movement,
an unpleasant experience for both of you. A final requirement is to
determine whether you are actually dealing with dirt. Plenty of times
I've chosen what I thought was the perfect location to create my six-
inch-deep latrine, only to find that a minuscule covering of duff was
camouflaging solid rock.

The act of early-morning exploration to find a place that is both
private, and comely, is one of intimate discovery. As you wander
around searching for the perfect place to dig, you find all sorts of
natural wonders that you wouldn't see otherwise: a crooked tree
clinging to an intriguing rock formation; thick, lime-green coats of
moss slathered on the side of a boulder; and lovely, little wildflowers
hiding in a teensy bit of meadow. Hopefully, what you don't find is
the toilet-paper white-flag evidence that someone else has the same
bathroom-choosing technique as you, or worse, witness a live perfor-
mance of No. 2.

On the other hand, at this fairly sophisticated dust bowl of a campsite, there was something special about the ability to head up to the pit
toilet and actually take a seat. So much less advance planning is necessary, and you don't even need to find your bright-orange "Beware,
I am going to take a dump in the woods" shovel. Even with the flies,
things just feel more comfortable when your bottom is planted on a
seat instead of holding on for dear life while you grip a rough piece
of granite and wonder whether someone will come along any minute
and introduce themselves. I keep forgetting to bring along a pair of
bike gloves to make that granite death grip slightly less painful to the

palms. Do you think I could market the gloves to backpackers if I changed the name to: Death Grippers? Granite Grabbers? Sphincter relaxers? Backwoods Bowel Mittens?

Once that task was completed, I hit the trail at seven o'clock. In the early-morning stillness, it was likely that not another soul was within five miles. Every day, the trail filled up with mountain bikers and hikers out for a quick trip on the Tahoe Rim Trail. Every morning, I was alone. It all makes sense since I'd only seen two thru-hikers in six days. The eastern half of the Tahoe Rim Trail is like a store that opens at nine o'clock in the morning and then at five o'clock in the afternoon, the sliding metal gate is brought screeching down and locked up for the night.

It was a short walk to Hobart Road, where I took a detour from the TRT, hiking past waves of lupine and paintbrush to the shore of Marlette Lake. Here a huge, flat rock sitting next to the shoreline provided the perfect opportunity for a glorious, finally get the infernal dust off my dirty body, swim, followed by another, and then a third equally satisfying dunking. There is really no way to adequately express the ecstasy one feels dipping your tired, dusty body into a mountain lake. One of the secrets to finding joy in backpacking is that you deprive yourself of material comforts, get really grubby and tired, and then, a swim in a lake, a cool drink, a serving of ice cream, a toilet, or a bed become spiritual experiences of rapture.

Calmly lying by the shore, blissfully relaxed, and filled with gratitude to be there, I should have spent the rest of the day at the lake. Instead it was barely lunchtime when I gathered my things, hoisted up my pack, and started walking. The damn infernal pull of my thru-hiker brain was striking again—the unyielding force that kept pulling me forward until I died or at least set up my tent. Even when you know where you are going and have only a few more miles to hike that day, this crazy, obsessive addiction still refuses to yield.

When I reached my little cabin in the woods, it was only two o'clock. Wait, I'm sure you're saying, "What the hell did he just say? Cabin in the woods? What happened to living in nature, making do with what the land gives you, depriving yourself of the luxuries of life to find spiritual joy?"

Opportunity arose. I knew the guy who owned these little cabins that were used by cross-country skiers in the winter and mountain bikers in the summer, and he just happened to have an opening when

I was rolling through. The Wild Cat Cabin was a tiny wood cabin tucked in a clearing in the woods set on a slope high above the trail. It had no running water or power, one small room downstairs, and a loft that barely had room for a bed. Just outside, a compost toilet. Water was limited to what a guy on a mountain bike could carry up the two steep miles from the road. But to this Day Six hiker, it was a Shangri-la. Well, at least it would be, as soon as I could figure out how to get in.

The key was apparently in the pocket of the last person who stayed there instead of where it was supposed to be hidden at the cabin. Shortly after I arrived, while I was considering various unattractive alternatives, all of which involved four more miles of walking, I could hear the water-delivery guy huffing up the last climb on his bike to resupply the cabin with water. He was almost as chagrined as me to discover that there was no key, so he turned around and pedaled back to Spooner Summit to see if he could find another key. I was kind enough to relieve him of his load of water, some of which I used to do my laundry while I awaited his return.

From the deck, I gazed at the filtered view of Emerald Bay, framed in an itsy-bitsy gap in the forest canopy. I pondered that view while waiting. And waiting. There was time to take a few lengthy dips in the useless pool of what-ifs-he-didn't return. Finally, I again heard the now-familiar heavy puffing as my rescuer made his way back up the last steep climb. Within minutes, I was lying on the couch and selecting a book to read.

This refuge in the woods was remarkably quiet except for an occasional creaking groan as the wood cabin flexed its muscles. While I was briefly excited to have a few of the basic comforts of home, soon being surrounded by a bit of civilization made me more lonely and bored than I would have been out in the woods. At times like these, you write crap like this in your journal: "Part of me seeks solitude, but when I find it, it can be a bit depressing. Why am I doing this grand adventure, and is it a success? Am I going bonkers, and will they have to put me in a straitjacket by the time I get done?"

But now I say to myself, "Geez, Louise! Buck up and quit whining. I won't put a straitjacket on ya, but perhaps duct tape across the mouth is in order."

I knew things were getting desperate when I began again pondering that four-mile round trip to the little store at Spooner Summit to get an ice cream and have a conversation that is not all inside my head. But I tried to not think about that and instead concentrate on reading *The Secret Life of Bees*. It was a pleasant distraction, but reading the entire cabin guestbook was more entertaining. It seems as if I was the only lonely hiker who had stayed there in recent years who had not come to the cabin to propose marriage, celebrate an anniversary, consummate a honeymoon, or just squank in the love nest, I mean, experience a lovely romantic encounter. There must have been at least eight marriage proposals made and accepted, and many more honeymoons and anniversaries. It was all a less-than-subtle reminder that I hoped the guy who comes up here and maintains this place disinfects that bed on a regular basis. Is it safe to put my sleeping bag on top of that thing? Where is that *CSI* black light to detect stray semen when you need it? Or perhaps it is best not to know.

The most interesting posts in the guestbook (yes, I had enough time to do a thorough analysis) were the reactions to the experience of getting here. The cabin is just a bit more than a two-mile walk from the parking lot at Spooner Summit. While there is a decent climb on a dirt road, it's no Mount Everest. Yet I read all sorts of drawn-out complaints about how far away it was, what a horrible walk it was, and "Oh, my God, I can't believe he took me *all the way* out here in the middle of the wilderness." (Maybe they were dragging one of those giant rolling suitcases; that would put a damper on things.) Now mind you, I'd just hiked sixty-four miles in six days to get to the relative luxury of this cabin to read diatribes from people whining about having to walk two miles, some of it uphill.

The highlight of reading the guestbook was a series of postings from the same guy over a two-year period. In the first posting, he goes on in detail about how beautiful it is at the cabin and how lucky they are to be able to spend this special time together at this peaceful spot in the woods. His companion, however, follows his heartfelt post with a protracted sniveling about how horrible it is and that she can't believe this scumbag brought her all the way out here to the boonies. Where it was, like, so boring. Oh, my God. A year later, the same guy is back. But this time, he writes about how he is so much happier because he is not up here with that pain in the ass whom he brought last year. The woman who is with him this year is actually enjoying their time together in the wilderness. It's all about perspective.

At sunset, I watched the light change to purple over the sliver of Emerald Bay while assessing my trip so far. I was getting more comfortable with the routine of walking. But once my camp was set, my stomach curdled and called out for companionship. Perhaps the European hut-to-hut experience is the proper way to hike. You spend the day hiking alone, enjoying the solitude. Then at night, you get together for food and pleasant conversation.

DAY SEVEN

I woke up the next morning refreshed after the first good night of sleep during the trip. It could have been because I was sleeping on a real bed or because of the darkness and quiet afforded by wooden walls instead of razor-thin nylon tent fabric. Outside, Emerald Bay was shrouded in mist, and the sky looked foreboding. A few patches of blue poked through as the light of sunrise arrived, but I prepared for wet. A family of deer was oblivious to my concerns, quietly munching on the tobacco brush just a few feet from the cabin.

Contrary to the diatribes of all those guestbook complainers, I found it to be just a quick jaunt to Highway 50. There I encountered the most dangerous obstacle on the trip: crossing four busy lanes of freeway. Cars were rushing by at seventy miles an hour piloted by drivers who were also texting, yelling at the kid in the back, and late for an appointment in Carson City. You know, the spectacular glory of civilization that I'd managed to avoid for the past week. I looked both directions, listened carefully for the rush of impending doom, and sprinted across the road, swiftly and smoothly like a gazelle running from a lion. In reality, with my heavy pack and my hiking poles, I probably looked more like Igor from *Young Frankenstein* speed walking with canes.

Then began a five-mile slog of a climb through a dusty forest of fir to South Camp Peak, where the entire lake unfolded below, highlighted by the wide-open mouth of Emerald Bay. The term "peak" in this case probably came from the same guy with a penchant for excessiveness who called Gray Lake a lake. South Camp Peak is actually the top of a mile-long, flat, mostly treeless ridge. It makes for a lovely meander with views the whole way, but a peak is the last thing it is. Near the end of the ridge, I set my tired butt down on a wood bench followed shortly thereafter by my tingling feet and legs plopping onto a boulder. I found gratitude for being there. I'm not sure if the gratitude was for the view, or that someone had put this bench here and my feet were no longer in motion.

Across the lake, I got a good reckoning of where I had been and what I still had left to complete. Far across the wide expanse of deep-blue water, I spied a teeny white dot on the brown slopes below Ward Peak. This was the humongous water tank that sits on a hill near my house. At first I was elated with the good news: that dot is tiny, I've walked a long way. Then shortly the bad news: that dot is tiny; I have a long way to walk. That's what happens when you walk in circles. The truth smacks you right in the face.

Spurred with the realization that at Kingsbury Grade I would have food, water, and perhaps most importantly, human contact, I arose from that lovely bench even though my screeching joints were calling out for lubrication. After a few shakes to limber up, I got my train rolling through a land carpeted with waves of pinemat manzanita. Sooner than expected, I was at the Kingsbury North Trailhead. The disadvantages of hiking faster than you estimated is that you have to wait for your rescuer. I used the time wisely by lying on a nice flat rock and settling into a nice savasana. My friend Denise startled me out of my slumber bearing gifts of water, a crisp luscious apple, chocolate-covered espresso beans, and a ride to the Kingsbury South Trailhead, which at that time was three and a half miles of up-and-down pavement away.

If someone ever asks you to help them out on a long hike by bringing in supplies, you can gain an amazing amount of positive karma points if you agree to do so. Your hiking friends whom you rescue will remember you fondly forever. There is a reason hikers call them Trail Angels. Because when they show up, it is like a gift from God. There is an added benefit if you provide these services to an outdoors writer. When he finally gets around to writing the story ten years later in what is sure to become a best seller, he will write glowing reviews about the experience.

I still wanted to get a few more miles in before darkness, so Denise had to leave her little duckling to waddle off alone into the wilderness. When you hike about fifteen miles, take a nap, and then have to begin hiking again up one of the steepest parts of the trail, it's a bit of a challenge. When a thru-hiker says something is a bit of a challenge, it means you should be prepared for a major gauntlet. It's like when you ask a really strong mountain biker about a trail and he says that it's "a bit technical." This means that you will be attempting to ride through a precipitous, cliff-edged boulder field with roots the size of tree trunks.

I started at the Kingsbury South Trailhead, which at that time climbed straight up a ski run. In case you are not a skier, this is a grueling ascent for a hiker late in the afternoon who is already exhausted and carrying a heavy pack with a full tank of water. By the way, if you are reading this as a guidebook to hiking the Tahoe Rim Trail, stop and buy the real guidebook. Seriously. I know just the right one. But what I can say here is that this section of the trail has been rebuilt since my venture. There is no longer a three-and-a-half-mile road section that you can beg a ride from your friend. Now you have to hike the new section, which includes lots of extra miles with some climbs thrown in for good measure. But it also dishes out some idyllic hiking with views of the lake, a sparkling stream to provide the only water in many miles, and perhaps most importantly, you no longer have to climb up that freaking ski run.

I stumbled up the steep trail, letting out little guttural grunts over each of the hundreds of boulder steps that were not designed for a guy whose legs are too short to buy normal pants. After two miles that seemed like ten, I made it to the South Fork of Daggett Creek as the sun set behind the mountains. I found a tiny, flat spot to camp a little past the creek on top of a ridge. Just in the nick of time I may add, since the rain started to come down softly as soon as the tent was up. Fortunately, it was just a rain teaser, my specialty, which provided a tinge of cloud enhancements to heighten the pinks and purples of the sunset.

Just as it was getting dark, as I read in my tent, I heard a crashing noise coming from a nearby grove of firs. The forest was thick, so I couldn't see anything, but I could hear the spine-tightening, sphincter-clenching sound of bark being ripped off a tree. Loud grunting noises and the crunch of swiftly snapped branches added to the commotion. Steeling myself for an impending bear confrontation, I dug deep to find my studly, tough-guy voice that would make that bear quake in his boots. I tried for a bass note as opposed to my usual tenor and yelled: "HEY…BEAR! YEAH, YOU! I'M HERE. GO AWAY!"

That should do it. There was a moment of silence, followed by more grunting, more tree ripping, more loudly cracked branches. Wait, was he getting closer? A wave of head-numbing adrenaline hit my brain, and I yelled again. More stridently. "BEAR! I'M HERE. YOU MUST LEAVE NOW!" I am sure this version must have sounded much more manly and that the bear couldn't detect the trembling in my voice. There was a brief pause, and then I could have sworn I heard him moan something that I interpreted as "Oh…OK… If I have to go, I guess I will." And the branch snapping and tree ripping came to a stop.

I exhaled, took a few deep breaths, and then remembered I was still just a few quick bear strides away from where the now-silent bear had been ripping trees apart. I was just a teensy bit curious about the bear's current whereabouts. I thought about moving to another location, but to take down a tent and find another place in the dark didn't sound like a viable alternative. Sleep didn't seem like an immediate option, either, since I didn't know whether the bear was waiting patiently just outside my tent. I had visions of the bear, sitting ten feet away, holding up his finger to his buddy while attempting to hold back a snicker, and saying, "Now, watch what happens when I make a little noise…hee, hee, hee."

The evening's final journal entry said: "Hopefully, this journal will continue tomorrow."

DAY EIGHT

It did. Sleep, on the other hand, was not on the agenda. Although I didn't hear the bear again, every squirrel stepping on a pine needle or mouse taking a poop was cause for alarm. I have chased away bears from the deck of my home numerous times, but something's different when you encounter them in the wild. At home, there is the opportunity for a quick retreat to a sturdy structure with four walls and a ready supply of noisemakers or objects you can throw at the bear. To a bear, the two very thin walls of a tent just seem like wrapping paper on the tasty treat inside. Aside from the fear of being dragged out of the tent and mangled, an irrational fear I know because of the basic timidness of Tahoe bears, I faced the more likely fear of losing a pack or all my food.

I remembered the story of a friend who was hiking on the Tahoe Rim Trail through the Desolation Wilderness. In the middle of the night, a bear sauntered into her camp, climbed up the tree holding her food bag, ripped it to shreds, wolfed down its contents, and rumbled off into the forest. So there she was—twenty hard hiking miles from civilization with all her food gone. Dizzy from hunger, she walked out without any food except a half-eaten GU energy pack that someone littered on the trail. Not exactly enticing sustenance for a twenty-mile hike, but apparently hunger beats the fear of unknown saliva.

When I was reading the journal in the Wild Cat Cabin a day earlier, it was interesting to see how many folks who do not normally see bears were longing for the opportunity to do so. After chasing one out of my next-door neighbor's house, however, I've seen the destruction they can cause: cabinets ripped off walls, leather couch slashed, refrigerator door broken, poop and pee splattered across the carpet. It was the second time in just a few weeks that a bear had broken into his house. The bruin bypassed the electric fence and boarded-up windows the owner had installed in a valiant effort to keep him out. Instead, it climbed up a tree to the second-floor deck and smashed through the window to get inside. The owner's next recourse was to cut down the trees to prevent a third incursion.

I have admiration and respect for bears; they are curious and fascinating creatures, but I also realize they can be troublesome. What I hate is when people give names to bears that they regularly see in the neighborhood. "Someone killed Sonny...I love Sonny. He was always in our neighborhood. He was such a sweet bear." Rule No. 1: if a bear is hanging out in your neighborhood enough that you actually give it a name, it's eventually going to get into trouble. Bears are supposed to be wild, not sitting at the picnic bench with Boo-Boo in Jellystone Park. Make sure you don't provide them access to food. And chase them back into the woods where they belong and can do what they like to do best: scare backpackers like me.

■ ■ ■

Meanwhile, away from my bear soapbox, I climbed up over Monument Pass to get my first up-close look at the startling visage of Freel Peak. It dominated the skyline, no longer a blip on the horizon that seemed so impossibly far away when I stood atop Relay Peak just a few days earlier. Soon enough, I was at Star Lake. It was Day Eight, and I'd finally reached the first really awesome, "Oh, my God, I have to swim in it, I'm so glad I am spending the night here" lake. You now might be asking yourself, wait a minute, didn't he go swimming in Marlette Lake? That doesn't count because I wasn't on the Tahoe Rim Trail. I was on a brief foray off the trail, also known in thru-hiking circles as cheating. So I can't talk about it. Yes, the water in Star Lake was cold. But it was worth every second to be immersed in joyful wetness.

After my swim, I pulled a John Muir and eavesdropped on the Clark's nutcrackers loudly flapping among the whitebark pines around Star Lake. Nutcrackers are raucous, grating, jay-sized gray and black birds that hang out at the same high altitude as whitebark pines. The nutcrackers' primary food is whitebark pine seeds. They spend the summer hiding thousands of these seeds all over the forest so that when winter comes, they can raid their stashes. Humans forget stuff all the time. While I've been occasionally accused that I have a birdbrain, actual birdbrains are even smaller, and thus they forget where they put those seeds. Some of those forgotten seeds become clumps of whitebark pine trees. The power of forgetfulness. Perhaps I could harness the power of my own forgetfulness for good. I know already it keeps me in shape, because wherever I go, I have to go twice.

Ancient hemlocks also like this frosty, high-altitude location. Covered from head to toe in dark-green needles, they are loaded with tiny, intricate cones and some sport skirts as wide around the base as the trees are tall. Equally elder western white pines, which finally turn a burnished red when they have lived for many decades, are also prolific here at over 9,000 feet. They spout long, narrow cones hanging high in the branches. While these antique behemoths look healthy and happy, it is likely that millions of potential trees tried and failed to live under these harsh conditions. In nature, only the very strong and very few survive to live a long life. Somehow humans have bypassed this requirement.

■ ■ ■

I listened to the wind roaring through the trees. A complicated symphony, rising and falling in volume with each gust. The trees are the musicians, with needles, branches, and the wind their instruments. Slowly the music lifts up, reaches a crescendo, then softly retreats before rising up again, getting stronger and stronger until, just when it seems impossibly loud, it dies back once more.

In eight days I'd covered almost ninety miles, slowly marching around one of the most beautiful lakes in the world. Every day had brought a new vision of my future, a new perspective on my past. I had listened to the stories of fascinating people, seen heart-stopping beauty, and in the middle of the night in Tahoe Meadows, restrained myself from flying out of my tent and tackling a runner who had the nerve to loudly help another semicomatose racer get through the darkness. I've had the bejeebies scared out of me by a bear, and I've faced periods of wrenching loneliness. Was I out there getting my shit together and making great strides toward developing myself as a person for the next phase of my life, or was I just going for a long, painful walk? Hell if I knew, but I wasn't sure whether I would know the answer to that question until my journey was complete—and probably not even then. Perhaps, the lesson I was trying to learn is that it's just about the walking.

Sometimes, if I am lucky and my brain shuts up, it truly becomes just about the walking. My only focus is the rhythmic sound of crunching footsteps playing a tune as they dance on down the trail. Walking then becomes moving meditation. It is no longer about distance and time, or thought; it's just moving steadily down the trail, observing the world peacefully as it passes by. The problem of course is that this meditative state is like a good golf shot: it feels amazing, but it doesn't often happen and you are not exactly sure how to make it happen again.

Moving meditation disclaimer: While flowing down a trail in a blissful state of moving meditation, it is quite easy to inadvertently pass trail intersections or your planned campsite. The good news is that meditation while hiking is considerably safer than meditating while driving, when you suddenly realize you have been driving the last ten minutes and have no idea where you are.

I head into the woods by myself to directly connect to nature, but this was one of those times I missed being the leader of a hiking trip. The highlight of guiding others is passing along the tales of the places through which you are traveling. Telling what you know to those who don't know is humans' most ancient method of transferring knowledge from generation to generation. For me, that means pointing out the florescent orange tiger lilies popping up near a streambed; or noting the sly coyote smoothly drifting across the meadow; or suggesting a route to conquer a craggy peak. Back in the cave person days, the wise ones shared more useful information, like don't touch that hot, orange thing on which your mom is cooking dinner, or don't eat that mushroom over there or you'll start drooling like your Uncle Brain Be Gone. Conveying knowledge is a rewarding part of guiding, but seeing what I have seen dozens of times through the eyes of those who are seeing it for the first time gives me a fresh outlook on the majesty of my familiar places.

Now, before you all rush off to become hiking guides, you should know that to be a guide also means lots of first aid training, hours of mundane paperwork, and complicated food organizing before the trip even begins. Before picking up clients, I wash a van as if I were going to sell it. Next, you need to somehow stuff hundreds of pounds of guide gear and clients' suitcases (which are supposed to be small, but are usually big enough for a six-week trip) into the van before driving it through busy, unfamiliar cities while eight people in the back are all asking questions at the same time. It means attempting to keep everyone happy throughout a weeklong trip packed with activities fraught with potential pitfalls, especially that quiet one who seemed perfectly content until you read her review that said, "They were not paying attention to me!"

Meanwhile, back by myself at Star Lake, I attempted to record some of my thoughts in a journal. But as all writers know, the most challenging part of writing is taking that great thought that's in your head and making it appear the same when it comes out on the page. Brilliance of thought does not necessarily translate into a brilliant sentence.

Someday technology may advance to the point that we will be able to instantly record what our consciousness is seeing and thinking. I hope I'm gone before that idea comes to fruition. While this concept might be a boon for writers, it would be the end of most relationships. When we are having discussions with our intimate partners, all of us analyze and reject a whole host of stupid thoughts before opening our mouths and letting words flow out. If this thought app came into being, all those crazy ideas would not be subject to getting filtered into the trash can where they belong. Ask your partner what would happen if every thought they had about you were available for you to see. Now look at the horrified expression on her face as she violently shakes her head and agrees that this app would be a very bad idea.

DAY NINE

Early morning and the lake was still. Clark's nutcrackers were still slumbering because otherwise they would have been continuing their customary caw caw chorus.

Later, as the sun was taking its last few hearty stretches before rising over the mountains, the first birds leisurely called out, becoming louder and more frequent as the light approached. They were like high-altitude roosters, heralding the arrival of morning, except quite a bit less obnoxious.

Just as I was ready to hoist up my pack for today's walk, a huge spider emerged from the top of the pack. It was so big that I knew immediately that an attempt to brush it aside with a Kleenex would just make it laugh. A large and sturdy shoe wielded with enough force to put a hole in the wall would be necessary. I made a frenzied effort to knock it off the pack, but it slithered inside and disappeared. All day as I hiked, I thought about that spider and wondered...where is it now? Was that a spider leg that just gently touched the back of my neck or just the wind? Perhaps it is safe and warm in the bottom of my sleeping bag, waiting to slowly crawl up my leg just as I am about to fall asleep tonight?

While spiders can occupy your mind part of the time, most of your hiking day is consumed with where you are and where you are going. Being present in the moment would seem to be an easy task while hiking, but just like in the rest of life it can be a trial. Instead, my mind thinks: well, if I hike to there by Sunday, I can get to there by Monday, which means by next Friday I should be finished.

In the present, however, it was an enchanting day for a hike. The first mile out of Star Lake is a magical journey through hearty white-bark pines and stunted wizard hat-topped hemlocks. High above sat the stark visage of Freel Peak, at 10,881 feet, the Tahoe Basin's highest peak. Far below lay the lightly shimmering plain of Lake Tahoe.

With rhythmic grunting, I made my way up the last two sandy switchbacks and over a late-season snow patch to Freel Saddle. At 9,700 feet, it was the highest place I'd been since Relay Peak five days earlier. From here, the spur trail to Freel Peak rises more than 1,100 feet in a mile. That's freaking steep. While most of the route to the top is barren sand with a few vestiges of snow, the trail passes through several groves of krummholz, stunted whitebark pine. When trees are in this state, they stay short but thickly spread over the ground, appearing more like bushes than trees. This low, sturdy profile allows them to withstand the brutal wind, cold, and deep snow they encounter on the exposed mountaintops.

I knew all this riveting information about the krummholz from several earlier summits of Freel Peak. There were too many miles yet to hike and too little energy in my legs to make the climb on this day. Instead, I sat on a bumpy boulder, shut my eyes, and fell into the still, peaceful sound of nothingness. I was in a place of bliss inside my head and soul that I didn't want to leave, but I still had thirteen miles to hike. I was still a thru-hiker on a mission. I roused myself from the silence, and I walked gently downhill through a scattered forest passing lush creeklets surrounded by thick batches of delphinium, lupine, and paintbrush. A few ancient junipers clung tight to the clefts between boulders. In the distance, the remains of blackened trees covered a vast slope, the result of the 2007 Angora Fire near South Lake Tahoe. It was a good place to be, and for a while the miles flowed quickly.

At Armstrong Pass, I began a long, switchbacking climb through enormous western white pine, lodgepoles, and red firs. While the trees were sparse, their huge shadows provided welcome relief from the painful ascent in the relentless sun. Near the top I ran into two thru-hikers who were going the opposite direction. I had briefly talked to them on my second day near Watson Lake. Since then, we had worked our way around opposite sides of the lake to meet again a week later. While I was hungry for communication, our conversation was short. They were upbeat and excited as they had almost completed their circle and would be off the trail that evening. Finally, I reached the Big Meadow Trailhead. I'd walked fourteen miles with enough ascent and descent to leave me exhausted, but it didn't feel that bad, at least it doesn't feel that way as I write this on my computer at home, quietly sipping a cup of tea and pondering whether I should have another piece of chocolate.

From the trailhead, I walked a quarter mile down a country road to a place romantically titled "Overflow Campground." It was free, unsupervised, just off the highway, and close to South Lake Tahoe, which I soon discovered made it a convenient place for the homeless or late-night ravers to congregate. Once I'd plunked my pack down, my first order of business was to find that damned spider. I donned gloves and slowly removed each item from the pack, holding it out gingerly at arm's length before giving it a brisk shake. With a wet forehead and a racing heart, I continued working my way through the contents, sure that the giant arachnid had to be in there somewhere. But I had no luck finding Charlotte's big brother. Even after the pack was empty and I'd given it a vigorous shake, no spider could be found. Where could it possibly have gone?

Just before dark, a car drove up and stopped at my campsite. A middle-aged woman emerged, and she said she was "in fire protection." But I noticed she was not wearing a uniform and her car was a very dirty, nondescript beater packed with a mishmash of possessions. It didn't look government issued, unless she was deeply undercover.

"The fire danger is really high, and I need to dismantle the firepits in all the campsites," she said authoritatively. "It needs to happen right away.... I can't believe we have gone this long before making it happen." She then proceeded to lazily remove one rock from my firepit and stopped to prattle on with her life story, or someone's life story. A steady series of contradicting accounts included the devil and at least one man who had done her wrong. Maybe I had hallucinated myself into a country song.

Later in the evening, I attempted to write down what she said, but I couldn't pinpoint any exact words. At the time, I was too busy trying to determine whether it was mind-altering substances that made her whacko or that she was just batshit crazy.

Either way, I started to think longingly of last night's campsite by Star Lake's shore. She finally removed a second rock from one side of the pit, placed it gently down on the other side, took a long look, rose up from the ground, waddled over to her car, and drove away. Whew. She needed a break. This firepit dismantlement business must be hard work.

Next up in the parade of campground characters was a guy who decided that three sites down from mine was an excellent location to repair cars. The gentle sound of the wind rustling through the fir trees was drowned out by the vroom vroom of an engine at full throttle spitting out puffs of smelly, gray smoke. Later, two huge guys started riding around and around the little loop that circles the campground on what appeared to be ancient miniature motorcycles. They looked like football players riding kids bikes...which of course they were.

Close to dark, two beat-up, old cars started slowly driving around the loop. They circled the campground very slowly twice, then drove out quickly, only to return a half hour later to repeat the procedure. Were they drug dealers or partiers wondering when the rave was going to begin? Perhaps they were just trying to locate their friend, the "fire marshal" for a resupply?

I stuffed plugs in both ears, brought the sleeping bag tight over my face, shut my eyes, and thought…"I wonder where is that spider?"

DAY TEN

On a long hike, eventually you get so damn tired you can even sleep through the shenanigans at the Overflow Campground and the adventures of the disappearing spider. When I arose in the morning, the campground was empty and the only-come-out-at-night circus parade had evaporated into the woods. I anticipated some great hiking: the wildflowers of Meiss Meadow, the shimmering waters of Showers Lake, and soon, the ravishing beauty of Desolation Wilderness. I was about to turn north to head onto what could be the best part of the hike, with just four days till home.

What I had felt as loneliness I was now attempting to convince myself was just boredom and a lack of skills at dealing with downtime. I was determined to feel in tune with nature and escape from the dregs of civilization via this two-week trip through a porthole into the wilderness. I decided to direct my focus to the gentle rhythm of the bird song, the permanence of the ancient trees, and the shimmer of water rippling across the lake.

■ ■ ■

The birds are a good place to start, because their background music is a constant companion as you hike. They chitter, chatter, and caw. They swoop and dive, bop and flutter, flashing brief glimpses of color as they flit through the brush. A quick shot of a blazing yellow and red western tanager. A woodpecker playing peekaboo around a tree. An osprey soaring smoothly overhead. We only get a few seconds to focus intently and try to absorb their beauty and style.

The Sierra's trees are always worthy of introspection as well. I've spent years in the woods marveling at them and never get tired of talking (or writing) about them. They range from spindly little lodgepoles and firs to the lonely and majestic junipers which cling to cliffsides, wresting their roots into tiny slivers in the rocks, cracking into the hard stone like walnuts in very slow motion. The higher the elevation, the more difficult it is to be a tree, but the challenges they face turn the ancient survivors into incredibly diverse and fascinating specimens that are loaded with individual personality and character. Every three-hundred-year-old Sierra tree looks different than all the others. The years twist them into odd angles and show the scars they have endured to live this long. They drop lower limbs while up high grow awkward branches that flail out in every direction, forming giant canopies. The bark of ancient Jeffreys, lodgepole, and sugar pine changes from the mottled gray of their youth to a rich, soft red with wide jigsaw plates. Young lodgepoles grow like corn stalks, narrow and tightly packed together. But at high altitude, the few hearty lodgepole survivors grow tall, truly distinct, and deserving of awe. Even after they die, the ancient behemoths of the cold, dry climates stand for decades, becoming smooth barkless monuments to the past. Their tall trunks twist to form artful patterns of dark lines on a stark canvas of smooth white.

In places where the soil is rich, vast ancient cathedrals of red fir are covered in carpets of lime green lichen. Their shadows leave the forest floor so dark it never sees the sun, while the prissy church lady in the back of the fir cathedral has been strictly enforcing the noise rules, as the red fir forest is oppressively silent.

I had walked one hundred miles and while there were certainly similarities, each bend in the trail, each pile of gray rock, craggy ridge, or wildflower-filled meadow was unlike the last. Every morning and every evening, I was lucky enough to witness the greatest show on earth. At daybreak, the curtain went up with just a hint of grayness. A dimmer switch spun in slow motion, little by little bringing more light to the world. The first calls of birds were heard, just as a high point to the west was first touched by the golden glow of sunlight. Then, oh, so very slowly, the sun's rays marched down the slope toward my camping spot. I knew it would arrive and bring light and warmth, but like everything else when you watch it too closely…it takes its sweet time. First, it lights up the tops of the tallest tree, then a tree to the left and to the right, and finally it lumbers down to my campsite, bringing a blast of warmth that lights up my face and heart.

Watching this show is better than being in the audience at any production, because here you are a part of the show. And then, at the end of the day, you get to watch it again, this time in reverse. The shade slowly rolls over the landscape, while the sun provides beautiful pinks, oranges, and at last, purple. To the east the glory of the sun still bathes the mountains in gold. It is a tragic comedy. A glorious heart warmer. And it happens twice a day. Meanwhile, at home we change the channel, perhaps catching a brief glimpse during the commercial or on our way to the bathroom as we cry out a hearty, "Hey, look, there's a great sunset."

Joe met me at the trailhead for my last food resupply. It was great to have a friend to talk to, although I was pushing my pace to the limit to keep up with him. He was a man of few words, so his fast pace was most likely a strategy to decrease the volume of my blabbering to background noise level. He was the same perky runner I'd run into on Day Three while I was climbing toward Relay Peak. On that day, he'd already clipped off ten miles while I was just beginning to catch my stride. Joe lived just down the street from me, so as we hiked he enlightened me on the latest happenings in the hood. While I had been gallivanting my way around the lake, the resident bears were slowly but surely bursting through doors and sneaking in windows in almost every home in the neighborhood. I was sure without me there to defend it, my castle would probably be next.

■   ■   ■

This is perhaps the best section of the Tahoe Rim Trail for wild-flowers. Low-lying Elephant heads dot lushly green Meiss Meadow, while lupine and paintbrush blanket the slopes below Showers Lake with sparkling waves of purple and orange. By early afternoon, I'd said goodbye to Joe and was immersed in the cool waters of Showers Lake, mulling my next move. In hindsight, I should have been content with my day and settled in for the night at this lovely lake. But noooo, I pressed on. Actually, perhaps I did have hindsight, because I would later discover that my head was up my ass.

My thought after leaving Showers' luscious waters was to camp somewhere in the bowl to the north of the lake. There, volcanic crags that look like castles from the Middle Ages guard a high ridge. Just below the ridge, huge cornices of snow form each winter, then in the spring and summer unleash dozens of tiny creeks that cascade down, feeding waves of shoulder-high lupines. The trail divides the dark-gray volcanic rock of the ridgeline and the smooth waves of polished pink granite sloughing toward the deep canyon below. I'd walked this bowl a dozen times and consider it one of the most magnificent miles on the Tahoe Rim Trail. The thought of camping there propelled my ass out of the lovely water of Showers

Sometimes, however, when you are actually trudging along trying to choose a spot to lay down the tent, the reality doesn't live up to the dream. It was a reality I had discovered while endlessly plodding up the miles through Humphreys Basin the year before, when I was heading for home after leaving the John Muir Trail. It seemed like a place that should have been chock-full of delicious tent sites, but I searched valiantly without any luck. Now, it was late afternoon, and this whole bowl north of Showers Lake was either sopping wet, loaded with thick vegetation, or sloped so unmercifully that a decent campsite couldn't be found. The next thing I knew, I'd climbed out of the bowl, and while gazing back at the beauty of what was behind me, found one last option. It was fairly level with a view back toward the dream bowl. Then I looked up. Just above the one place to pitch a tent, I found a long-dead, precariously leaning tree. Would tonight be the night it finally fell?

I then walked down the trail and into a hiking twilight zone. Stuck on a treadmill where nothing looks like a good place to camp, I become incapable of actually putting the pack down. It's the hiker's equivalent of driving by one gas station or restaurant after another while failing to pull the damn car off the road. You know, a dad move. Dads keep thinking that the price will be lower at the next station or a better restaurant must be right around the corner. Or I'm in the fast lane, "Oops, there went the turnoff." We just keep driving until the noise from the back seat finally rises to the point that we have no alternative. We have to pull over, even if it is at a place that is clearly inferior to all the other choices we could have made but passed by.

Twilight was moving swiftly toward Too Damn Dark to Put up a Tent, and I was stuck in the fast lane, nothing passing my warm and fuzzy tent site test. Finally, the kids in the back of my head were demanding that I pull over. Now! I ended up in a semi-flat, pine cone-laden site just above a boggy, buggy meadow. It was a depressing way to end what had been a day of skipping my way happily through a land of natural splendor. I ruminated on the lesson I was learning: you must stop when you should stop; otherwise, you will stop where you shouldn't stop because you just have to stop.

Exhausted in my tent, I relished that the Tahoe Rim Trail and Pacific Crest Trail had joined on this day, and I began to run into a steady march of hearty PCT thru-hikers making the 2,600-mile trek toward the Canadian border. PCT hikers begin their journey by hiking for weeks through the scorching Southern California desert, then climb into the 500-mile-long High Sierra, where they must sur-mount passes over 13,000 feet covered under deep snow well into June. Most years, there is just a short four-month window between the time when the trail fully emerges from the snow and when it is covered again with the next winter's deep blanket of white. If they start too early, when they reach the High Sierra, hikers will not be able to find the trail under the snow, be prone to slide down steep slopes on the ice, or be swept away by an avalanche. As the tempera-tures rise and the snow finally begins to melt, hikers face another chal-lenge: hundreds of bridgeless streams, laden with roaring snowmelt, making for a dangerous, deep, and cold crossing. Ah, but if you wait too long, your hike through the Southern California desert will be brutally hot and water will be in even shorter supply. Then after sur-viving a couple thousand miles of desert and high mountains, you might get caught in a blizzard in the mountains of Washington with several feet of snow putting your life in danger.

To complete the PCT in 130 days, you have to average more than twenty miles a day. That is a lot of long days. How much persistence and determination do you need to successfully thru-hike the PCT? I heard this story from one of the thru-hikers I met: A woman hiked several twenty-five-mile days so she could make it to Truckee, Califor-nia, in time to get to the bookstore there by midnight, when the latest Harry Potter book was being unveiled for purchase. Then, first thing the following morning, she returned to the trail and began hiking again. That's right, she hiked with a two-pound book in her pack. While an additional two pounds for a book is an unnecessary burden for any hiker, thru-hikers are incredibly anal about every ounce of weight that they carry on their backs for hundreds of miles. She was probably a person who sawed off half her toothbrush to save weight. This book occupied her brain while she read it, but it also occupied some prime real estate in her pack. Apparently, she was partial to Harry Potter.

The previous week, while I was walking among the rad bike dudes, the flip-floppers, and the gapers, I'd stood out as a real backpacker with my bigger-than-a-kids' school pack and semi-crusty look. Now, with ten days under my belt, I looked as fresh as a baby compared to the mega thru-hikers who'd been hiking for seventy days. They talk months, not weeks. They talk in hundred-mile segments, not fifteen-mile segments. These hikers are generally thin, wear clothes that look dirty but are perfectly functional, carry a light pack, and have scruffy-looking beards. They each have a trail name. I met Cash Aye and Steely Dan. Cash Aye was given his name because he referred to water caches as "cash ayes," like they were French. I can sympathize. I remember in high school looking at a college course catalog and wondering what I pronounced as a "pre request e" was.

Thru-hikers are generally amicable, willing to help each other out whenever help is needed. But they are overwhelmingly focused on ticking off the miles, trying hard to reduce the number of zero days, when they did not accumulate any miles. Zeros need to be made up somewhere, so they are kept in reserve for a very special occasion. Future zero days become carrots, leading the tired hiker on to the promised land of such incredible luxuries as restaurant food, a shower, a bed, and even more restaurant food. Pizza and beer are big. Ice cream is another food drug of choice. But each hiker has their own obsession. In her acclaimed book, *Wild: From Lost to Found on the Pacific Crest Trail*, Cheryl Strayed talks about obsessing over a cold Snapple Lemonade while she was hiking the PCT. Whatever keeps your brain occupied so your body keeps clicking off the miles.

DAY ELEVEN

One advantage to the extra dad miles I hiked on Day Ten was that I was now closer to Lower Echo Lake, and more importantly, the Echo Chalet. Of course, the concept of mileage hiked today is mileage I don't have to hike tomorrow is the sort of insidious logic that keeps dads hiking long after they should have set up camp. Fortunately, I arrived at the rustic Echo Chalet store at lunchtime, where something extraordinarily magnificent was placed in front of me: a sandwich. Ham on rye with fresh lettuce, tomato, cheese, avocado, mayo, mustard, and peppers—with only the avocado being something I had eaten in the last eleven days. Until you have been on the trail for ten days, you cannot begin to understand the profound rapture experienced by the over-freeze-dried taste buds of a hiker when that first bite of crispy, crunchy lettuce or juicy, red tomato hits the mouth. But wait, there's more: an ice-cold sweet beverage followed by the pièce de résistance, ice cream. Real ice cream, with chunks of chocolate in it, melting gloriously in my mouth.

As I lingered in my food stupor, I listened to the stories coming from the small collection of thru-hikers next to me who were also cramming copious quantities of food into their mugs. They looked like Civil War soldiers on the long and hungry journey home after the war had ended. Battle hardened and wiry, they had just arrived at the home of a supporter who was willing to take them in and give them their first decent meal in a month.

Eventually, I dragged myself up from my little piece of paradise, because that is what thru-hikers do, and started the rocky walk up to Tamarack Lake. My plan for Tamarack, as of two weeks earlier, was to meet friends with whom I would spend the night. I was excited that it would be my first chance on the trip to spend the evening talking with someone besides myself. I set up my tent and kept popping my head up like a prairie dog every time someone walked by, only to slump back down when I realized it was not my friends. They never showed up.

I did, however, see lots of other people. The place was teeming with humanity ensconced in every potential campsite around the lake. Since I waited and waited for my friends to show up before setting up my tent, the only site I could find was a narrow strip of dirt tucked in tight between a pile of sharp rocks a good distance from the lake. My "campsite" was treeless, baking in the afternoon sun, and the walk to the lake required some tricky dance moves over loose stones and pointy boulders. Desolation Wilderness in the middle of the summer can be a busy place, and Tamarack Lake either was chockablock with illegal campers or the quota of allowed hikers is way too high. It was a freaking zoo that felt less like a lake in the wilderness than a campground along Tahoe's midsummer shore. As I reclined in my tent alone, I heard the zoo of characters along the lakeshore, but they didn't provide me with any conversation or camaraderie.

■ ■ ■

Desolation Wilderness is like the pretty girl in high school. Although all the other guys are stumbling all over themselves to be with her, you just can't resist giving it a shot yourself. Ralston Peak's pyramidal mass of dark-gray rock stood loftily above Tamarack to the south, while Echo Peak's mass of smooth granite dominated the view to the north. Sure my campsite was meh, but my day included a refreshing dip in Upper Echo Lakes' chilly clear waters as well as an end-of-the-day dunking into the sparkling waters of Tamarack. Even with the crowds, I can't resist a Desolation Wilderness lake. The craggy shoreline winds past knobby pines clinging to life in tiny crevices. Offshore, granite islands topped with hearty bonsai trees beckon me into the water. And rising up from the shore's edge, an alluring mountain ridge reaches toward a craggy, treeless summit.

DAY TWELVE

There I was, smack in the middle of the best that Desolation Wilderness had to offer, at the edge of Dicks Lake at six in the evening, lying on my pad peacefully pondering my fortune to have experienced a three-swim day. To those of you in the civilized world, that's equivalent to a five-star hotel or a four-star restaurant.

The day began with a mile-long climb toward Lake Aloha over a barely there trail that was a mishmash of rocks and boulders. I kept rolling my ankles on the unevenly sloped and precariously spaced stones while getting my hiking poles stuck in the holes between the rocks. When not fully concentrated on correctly landing my next foot plant, I was thinking of two things: wow, these views are amazing, and, wouldn't it be awesome if a crew of prison inmates would spend a couple weeks smashing the shit out of these damn rocks so they wouldn't hurt my poor tootsies.

By midmorning, I'd reached Lake Aloha, which stretches out across the wide-open plain of Desolation Valley and ruts up against the massive ridge of granite known as Crystal Range. This long ridge of solid rock heads north from Pyramid Peak, climbs precipitously from Aloha's western shore, and is the backbone of Desolation Wilderness. Dozens of rock islands fan across Aloha's surface, while onshore, just a few stunted and twisted trees break up the desolate expanse of water and stone. At first glance, the Hawaiian word "aloha" seems like a strange moniker for a high mountain lake that is frozen over much of the year. But if you climb high above the lake on a sunny summer day, the water and islands do look a bit like a tropical paradise.

Lake Aloha, however, is a moody bugger. If you arrive on a warm windless day, early enough in the summer that the lake is full, it's prime swimming terrain. Lake Aloha, however, has a dam. And the El Dorado Irrigation District lets the water out of Aloha, Caples, and Echo Lakes into the South Fork of the American River, usually in a rush around Labor Day. If you arrive in October, you may find yourself plodding along a much smaller lake, hunched over in a desperate attempt to stave off the biting cold and howling wind. Fortunately, this was one of the good days. I immersed myself in its translucent water and was in no hurry to get out. I watched tiny bugs swarm through the water like a school of fish in the soft morning light. They swooped and turned, some unseen force sending them rapidly in one direction then quickly off in another, all following the leader, or whomever had the gumption to go in a different direction.

■ ■ ■

On the smooth granite, I waited patiently for the sun to warm my skin. The wind was still, so I could just hear the distant tumbling of talus down the slopes of Pyramid Peak. It was a good time to write:

> My trip has been more difficult emotionally than physically. When I focus on the beauty and tell myself how lucky I am to be here, it is easier. A part of me longs for companionship, but perhaps I'm learning more about myself and growing more as a person by doing it alone. The days are long, and it is when I have too much time in camp that I ponder my loneliness. If I don't want to spend my afternoons twiddling my thumbs, I need to stop and swim. To linger over lunch and to quietly witness the magnificence of this trail. If we give ourselves time for placid reflection, we can appreciate not only the big picture—the massive peaks still holding patches of snow and the shimmering blue waters of the mountain lakes—but also the more intimate experiences, like an individual giant juniper holding tight to a little gap in the rocks, or multicolored lichens marching up the side of a cliff.

Aloha asked me to stay and keep writing, but I still had some hefty miles and a pesky pass to complete, so even with my newfangled plan of delaying getting to camp, I had to leave her, promising to return some day soon. The trail leaves Aloha and descends through giant, vibrant red and gray rocks that have tumbled down from the lofty slopes of Jacks Peak. Bustling creeklets rattled through patches of heather, paintbrush, and tiger lilies, then dropped to a lusciously green meadow. The last vestiges of winter snows fed cigar roll-shaped corn lilies just escaping from the muddy earth. Then Heather Lake: translucent blue, shining like a diamond in the midst of stark granite and metamorphic wonder. Just past Heather, the lake's outlet creek disappears into a narrow ravine, where a ten-foot-high, fifty-foot-long snow tunnel forms each spring over the creek bed. Inside the drippy tunnel, the bluish-white snow formed geodesic shapes like an upside-down golf ball.

Swim No. 2 was at Susie Lake. I flopped around joyously in the cool water, then sat on the red rock bordered shoreline to ponder, or try to avoid pondering, my clearly visible next goal: Dicks Pass. What makes the pass clearly visible is that it sits on the high ridge between the lofty summits of Dicks Peak and Mount Tallac. It's an impressive front, effectively dividing Desolation Wilderness in two, and from Susie, looks like a bitch of a climb. The hike begins with a half-mile descent because it is always good to make the climb longer and more difficult. Some whining aside, it's only a 1,600-foot climb. And it's so damn pretty and well laid out that it's actually an enjoyable ascent. Once you start up the long traverse, you've got these glorious views of Dicks and Jacks Peaks, with Half Moon Lake and Alta Morris Lakes seemingly at your feet. Occasionally an ancient juniper or whitebark pine provide shade from the stark landscape, and a few waves of bright-orange paintbrush and purple lupine lend color wherever a bit of water seeps up through rock.

Then, certainly not quite before I knew it, but not exactly after going through hell either, I reached the top, where a perfectly placed car-sized flat rock was waiting to accept my posterior. I must have contemplated life on that particular platform at least a dozen times, and except for that one time it has always done me well…fade to blurry dream sequence with voices that sound far away…

■   ■   ■

That one time I was sitting with friends on the top of Dicks Pass, ravenously plowing through peanut butter and jelly sandwiches and savoring the expansive view when we noticed a threatening cloud. It was way the hell off in the distance, so we just thought it added a bit of variety to the already impressive view. A few minutes later, though, it didn't seem so far away anymore. Soon we could see rain pouring out of what now had mushroomed into a much larger cloud, and it was rapidly heading in our direction. Shortly after the first lightning strike, we came to the logical conclusion to head down. Quickly. Sitting in the open at the top of Dicks Pass perfectly fits the description of where lightning experts say you should not be in a lightning storm.

We'd just barely begun our descent when rain and hail began viciously pelting us. Ear-splitting cracks of thunder and lightning rattled over our heads. If you think you can't hike any faster with a backpack on, start hiking down from a ridge when the lightning is flashing right above and the hail is starting to sting as it pings your head. This tends to focus the mind and body and shifts you into a whole new gear for speed. Eventually, drenched and shivering with both cold and fear, we made it into the relative shelter of the forest.

■ ■ ■

Meanwhile, back on Day Twelve. The views to the south from my smooth rock on this cloudless day were enticing and relaxing. No impending doom cloud forced me down the hill. I took a quick excursion north to the other side of the ridge and was treated to equally impressive views of Dicks Lake, Fontanillis, and the three Velma lakes.

Then there it was. Twin Peaks. Still a good ways off, but within the realm of distance someone could walk to in a few days. Home. In the far horizon to the northeast, I could just barely see Mount Rose, just down the ridge from Relay Peak, where I walked eight days earlier. Holy shit, this is a long hike. What ignorant fool agreed to hike this whole thing? And at 170 miles, it's pretty wimpy compared to the Pacific Crest Trail. I am only hiking about nine hundred thousand feet or about three hundred thousand steps, while those who hike the PCT must walk more than thirteen million feet or more than five million steps? Preposterous. And those who complete the task don't win a million dollars, get lauded on TV, and garner three million Instagram followers. They just get the mental satisfaction of accomplishing an extremely challenging goal that most people don't care about or understand. Are they are out of their freaking minds?

As I calculated all these long distances and patted myself on the back for being such an amazing hiking stud, two runners coming from the north popped up to the top of the pass. They looked quite refreshed. Like they had just played a set of tennis, but still had enough energy for a sprightly game of croquet after they pick up Buffy and Biff from camp. They were out for a quick run of the entire thirty-two-mile section of the TRT from Barker Pass to Echo Lake and had already run twenty-two miles. Just ten more to go, with most of the uphill completed. Yep, there it is again: life giving me the opportunity to put my accomplishments in perspective. There is always someone, and perhaps lots of someones, who can do it better, faster, farther, and with a smile on their face like they are hardly winded. Those assholes—I mean, those inspiring people. Of course, the question is: are they inspiring me, or like the Sirens of Greece, enticing me to take on challenges above my pay grade.

The northside walk down to Dicks Lake was a smooth roll through a thick forest of hearty hemlocks with frequent glimpses of my glittering lakeside destination. Soon enough, I was camped at Dicks' prime camping spot just above the lakeshore. After spending the previous night as the new arrival at a crowded zoo, tonight I was the only one camping at Dicks. It's amazing how much smarter you feel when you arrive on a Sunday night instead of a Saturday. I ran into some folks from Tahoe City who had hiked over from their camping spot at Middle Velma Lake to take a dip into Dicks. We swam together in the crystal-clear water. It was wonderful just spending an hour having a lively conversation with some folks from home, but when they got ready to go I wished they could stay longer. Instead, I was once again alone in the wilderness. If you don't want to be alone, you need to bring other people with you, I reminded myself. But where would I find such people? And why am I asking you?

To keep the conversation with other humans going, I walked up to the saddle near Tim's Knob to make a phone call home. Tim's Knob is a rocky crag above the saddle near Dicks Lake where the PCT and Bay View trail meet. A quick scramble to the top provides views of all of Fontanillis Lake, which spreads out long and narrow, winding its way through the granite, as well as the three Dicks: Lake, Pass, and Peak. It was very unofficially "named" Tim's Knob many years ago by a group of hikers whom I led to the top. Apparently, they were feeling guilty for having stuffed my pack with rocks and their empty lunch bags while I was busy relieving myself in the trees. If you stuff a guy's pack with little rocks, the least you can do is name a big rock after him. And if you are a writer, the least you can do is write a paragraph in your book that mentions the name Tim's Knob four times. Awesome.

I was able to reach my daughters on the phone, and as opposed to my three-day trips, on Day Eleven of this long journey, they were actually quite excited to hear the stories of Dad's adventures. They might even have expressed a teensy hint of pride. I was happy to hear their voices, but when I hung up, the lofty drug of communication quickly began to wear off, and the comedown left me feeling worse than before I called. Only a few days to go. There is just too much stuff to pack into this one, short life. Whatever you are doing, you miss what you are not doing.

Just before dark, I heard a loud splash in Dicks Lake. It sounded like someone or something jumping into the lake, but I didn't think that anyone else was around. Was there a rather large animal quickly headed in my direction via a brisk swim across the lake? I tiptoed my way down to the water, wondering what monstrous creature I would find, and sat on a boulder at lake's edge. The last rays of sunshine showed golden reflections in a million tiny ripples. All around were gentle, circular plops as dozens of fish jumped…then, another loud splash! I jerked my head to see an osprey's wings fighting for purchase as it slowly lifted out of the water, a fish held tight in its talons. It then glided away toward its nest on the other side of the lake. A few minutes later, the osprey was back for another dive, before settling back into its nest for the evening. Through the trees, one last golden-red stripe of sun slowly dropped below the mountaintop, leaving the osprey and me alone in the quiet, headed toward darkness.

DAY THIRTEEN

In the morning, the sun kissed Dicks Peak first, then marched slowly down the steep slope, rays setting tree after tree aglow in a fire of gold. Tall dead trees glow white in the morning sun, standing proudly years after life is gone. Whiter even than the shining barkless trees are the last patches of snow hanging on to the face of Dicks Peak. Gentle waves lap against Dicks' rocky shoreline, sounding like the lake is laughing, happy to see another day.

I hear the osprey cheeping, but not hunting. Probably belching, still attempting to digest last night's impressive fish feast. It waits patiently throughout the day for the time just before dark when the hunting is perfect. The fish have waited throughout the day for the perfect time to hunt the fly, and the fly feels that twilight is the perfect time to come down and rest on the surface of the lake. For many, it is a short nap, as the entire food chain happens in a second as the fly touches the lake, the fish grabs the fly, and the osprey plucks the fish.

Even though I spent quite a bit of time enjoying the sunrise show, frost still clung to the outside of my tent by the time I packed up and hit the trail. Apparently, I had walked from summer into fall. Almost immediately I was hit by a loud, raucous flap, flap, flap of flight of a grouse flushing just ten feet away. I've been startled by the flush of a blue grouse dozens of times, and it never ceases to make my head light up as a wave of adrenaline rush courses through my body. It is just too loud and happens so unexpectedly that my mind doesn't have time to figure out what in the hell that racket is. The chicken-sized blue grouse (a species which has now been split into two groups, with the sooty grouse version being the one we see in the Sierra) has no problem hanging out in trees or on the ground just a few feet away from humans. But then suddenly for some reason, they decide you are a danger and fly away like a flamethrower has just shot up their butt. After all that flapping and fluttering, they stop just a few feet away, turn around in circles a few times, look around puzzled like they are trying to figure out how they got there, then settle back down, apparently having no idea they had just made a big fuss about something. Someone watching a sooty grouse must have invented the term bird-brain. They are the Dory, from *Finding Nemo,* of birds.

I breezed past Fontanillis, always one of my favorite Desolation lakes, with its granite islands and Dicks Peak backdrop, then plunged into a dark forest of red fir that descends to Middle Velma Lake, perhaps Desolation's most popular lake. A set of tiny intriguing tree-topped islands are scattered around the lake, including one whose rock formation makes it appear like the Sydney Opera House. But every summer weekend, poor Middle Velma Lake is beaten down by hordes of hikers for whom Desolation Wilderness only means Middle Velma Lake. When hiking north on the TRT, however, it is the last good swimming lake for about one hundred miles, which might as well be forever.

After Middle Velma, the crowds thinned out immediately, with only a few scattered PCT thru-hikers willing to venture onto the next less-than-thrilling fifteen-mile slog north to Barker Pass. I found myself once again falling prey to the thru-hikers' "miles hiked today are miles I don't have to hike tomorrow" mentality. I took just a brief break at the warm and smelly Richardson Lake before chugging on. As usual, my mile obsession found me walking into impending darkness wondering where in the hell I was going to camp. I finally gave up at a dusty spot just down the trail from Miller Creek. Waiting for me were the mosquitoes. All of them. What is it about skeeters that they wait until you are most vulnerable to swoop in? You don't see them when you sit down to start filtering water; they wait to make their appearance until just the moment both hands are busy. That point when swatting at them means dropping the clean end of your water filter into the unfiltered water. Taking a leak? They wait until you are midstream, when there is nothing you can do about it but attempt to not pee on yourself and slap at the little suckers at the same time. I heard a rumor that women have an unfair advantage in mosquito management while peeing. They have two free hands.

Chased into my tent by the little bastards, I had time to think about how my journey would be over the next day. I was terribly anxious to get home, but also realizing I would miss the simple life on the trail. Out there in the so-called civilized world they have people, lots of them, making noise and talking. There would be appointments, assignments, and things that had to be done at a certain time. It was beginning to sound suspiciously like work.

I reflected on what I learned on this trip: when you are hiking alone in the woods, you have to find a way to reconcile who you are and be comfortable with yourself. While I understood that was the goal, I certainly hadn't yet discovered how to accomplish it.

Spending time by yourself is hard. But it forces you to make connections. To step out of your comfort zone, reach out, and make the effort to meet other people and learn their stories. While you may not bother to care about those stories if you are hiking with other people, when you are solo, they become your primary focus and an outlet for your fears. A surprising value of hiking alone, then, is that you instantly become more interested in what other humans are doing. On this trip when I made the effort to stop and talk to people, I learned about the intricacies of gay adoption, being a photographer for a major newspaper, thru-hiking Russian refugees, bilingual children learning about backpacking, and what it is like to fight wildfires. When I had my mind and eyes open, and my mouth shut, I learned that nature could teach me about diving ospreys, the incredible resiliency of trees, the vastness of space, and the never-ending march of the sun.

What I have learned about myself is still an open question...and I'm sure it will be the question I will be asking for the rest of my life. I read somewhere that we all are living our lives as first drafts. All we can do is just keep trying to revise and improve. Or perhaps whether we like it or not, we are all still living the life of a sixteen-year-old: excited about what life will bring us but anxious to get it going already.

DAY FOURTEEN
The last day.

When my smelly, dirty, sore body finally made it to Barker Pass, I collapsed onto the smooth wood surface of a picnic bench overlooking Blackwood Canyon and Lake Tahoe, and I thought about the changes that were about to happen when I returned to "real life." Every time I say the phrase "real life," I think of that YouTube video that was popular a number of years ago: "David after Dentist." In it, little seven-year-old David, future philosopher, ponders life after his trip to the dentist while still under the influence of a healthy dose of laughing gas. He looks at his dad seriously and asks, "Is this real life?" Yep. I know it is surprising sometimes, but this is it. And you may not know this yet, David, but it moves pretty damn fast…except when you are backpacking of course.

While the hiking was relentless and demanding with a pack that always seemed impossibly large, the hiking was actually the easy part of this trip. It was the icing on the cake. The reward we receive for spending those nights of loneliness, waiting in the darkness for sleep to come.

I stopped at the North Fork of Blackwood Creek for my last meal on the trail just a few miles from the end of my journey. There the wildflower-bordered creek dribbles down through a lush meadow, then drops steeply toward distant Lake Tahoe. I savored the woods, feeling content for completing my goal, while realizing that we only truly appreciate where we are when we are almost not going to be there anymore.

The last few miles, my mind was joyous with the satisfaction of accomplishing this demanding goal. My feet, on the other hand, thought my brain was full of crap and it was well past time to end this madness. They wanted to be sitting somewhere doing absolutely nothing. My hips and their close partner in pain, my butt, chimed in as well, lobbying aggressively for a comfy chair. My body was beat to a pulp. Done. Kaput. Enough already. It had done its best to keep a stiff upper lip throughout the journey, but now that the trip was over, it screamed, "What in the hell have you done to me?" I was like a dog that chases every squirrel in the forest all day long and then as soon as it jumps into the truck, passes out and is useless for the rest of the day.

■ ■ ■

A few days later, I hiked up to Stanford Rock. From there, sitting majestically atop the Sierra crest just a mile away was the rocky massive of Twin Peaks. A few small patches of snow still held on to its north-facing slope. While Twin Peaks is a grand spectacle from this close, it is also just another blip of the thousands of rocky protrusions that make up the crest of the Sierra. One could hike every day for a dozen lifetimes and never see all of them, but on this trip, this little mark on the ridge was my place marker, which told me how far I had gone and how far I still had to go. And most of all, it kept telling me that I can hike a long ways in two weeks.

In fourteen days, I had gained a new sense of connection with the power of nature. As we marvel at the beauty of the natural environment, we tend to glorify her for her power and majesty. We are relaxed and rejuvenated by her splendor. We find bliss and peace in her quiet. But when we finally spend a few weeks deep in her clutches, we begin to understand that nature really doesn't care about us. It is not a therapy class to repair us from what the civilized world has done to us. If you are stupid or unlucky enough to fall off a rock, you would get hurt, but nature would just go on. Equally important, it doesn't set out to hurt us. Nature is a neutral bystander. An enormous and spectacular canvas where all the plants and animals are continually revising the image. When a fly drops down to the lake, then gets gobbled up by a fish, who shortly thereafter is snatched by the talons of an osprey, nature is not out to get anything. It is just a big web of connections, all dependent upon each other. It's the place where plants and animals go about their daily quest for the three basic necessities of life: food, shelter, and sex. Every quest for food creates a winner who gets to eat and a loser who gets eaten. But every winner loses eventually, and the cycle continues infinitely. In our human society, we act like death never occurs. But in nature, it is an everyday occurrence, and blithely called the food chain.

My daughters used to enjoy saying, "Dad, it's not all about you." I grudgingly agree, but they didn't have to be such little shits about it. We can appreciate what nature has to offer us, but it is not a health spa designed to take care of our every need. I think I intuitively understood this, but when I got the chance to spend an extended period of time in nature, I felt it more strongly. And that is not a bad thing.

Perhaps we glorify nature because the break between the natural world and the civilized world is both dramatic and stark. And the way we live our lives is making this gap between the two worlds even larger. Perhaps my purpose on this planet is to introduce a few people to the natural world, so they can understand the separation, and learn to live their own lives with more balance.

I also sometimes reached that state of moving meditation. The miles, and even the loneliness, brought relaxation and inner peace. While I was walking, my brain would rest. My thoughts became simple and more directed at the basic needs of life. Once you reach that state of meditation, you begin to go back in time. A time when the human walk through life was about meeting your basic needs: the next meal, keeping warm, finding companionship, finding yourself, finding your purpose.

■ ■ ■

A few days after my trip, I brought my kayak down to the shore of Lake Tahoe and paddled a half mile out onto the lake. It was an utterly still morning, the water a mirror, reflecting the deep-blue sky. Except for the dull hum of a distant motorboat, there was silence. I slowly spun the kayak around in circles, taking in the ridgeline that sits high above the lake. I was encircled by my journey. It seemed impossibly big and undoable, but it was done. I had put one foot in front of the other until the task of walking all the way around this amazing lake was completed. What more can you ask of yourself?

Wind swept hemlocks at the base of Twin Peaks.

Cousin Cindi and I at the start of the Superior Hiking Trail. Little did I know what I was getting myself into.

What Days One, Two, and Three looked like on the Superior Hiking Trail.
Shoulda brought a machete.

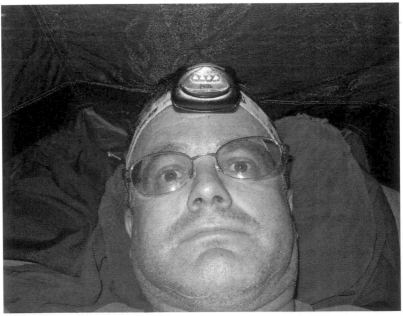
In my tent wondering what the hell I've gotten myself into.

Along the shores of Lake Superior.... It's colder than it looks.

The highlight of the trip.

Sunrise at Lake Agnes—yee haw, now we're talkin'.

Early morning at Fontanillis Lake—this is why I carry a backpack.

Kalmia Lake and Lake Tahoe from the Dicks Peak Ridge—so close to home, but so far away.

5

The Superior Hiking Trail...
Solo Hiking, Minnesota Style

The dark timber still sounded with their whine, their proboscises
were still alarmingly large and powerful. With every swat,
I splattered a dozen bloody bugs over pants and shirt.
An ordinary mosquito can penetrate the tough sputum of a
rattlesnake, but Northwoods species can pierce the rind of stones.

—William Least Heat-Moon

SUPPOSE I CAN BLAME IT ON the *Thru Hiker's Guide to America: 25 Incredible Trails You Can Hike in One to Eight Weeks,* by E. Schlimmer. For it was in that book that I first heard about the Superior Hiking Trail. The author spoke about this incredible trail along the shore of Lake Superior, America's largest lake. He went on at length about its excellent maintenance and camping opportunities and wrote that "the readers of *Backpacker Magazine* flatter the SHT like no other trail in existence...and overall it was voted the second-best long-distance hiking trail in the United States."

I was looking to get back into the woods after my successful thru-hike of the Tahoe Rim Trail. To hike solo once more, to experience the fulfillment and pride I felt while conquering the Tahoe Rim Trail, and to finally learn how to replace the empty, lonely feeling in my soul with satisfaction and peace that I am doing what I should be doing right now.

Based on the book's description, I assumed that the Superior Hiking Trail would be the perfect place to hike. It certainly seemed that hiking 235 miles in upper Minnesota, a place I had never been, would be an interesting way to spend a few weeks. I was not aware, obviously, that I was completely out of my mind to even consider hiking more than two hundred miles by myself in a place I had never been, and in the land of Lake Wobegone of all places. (By the way, if after reading my sterling account of the trail, you decide you need to run out and thru-hike this puppy right away, allow extra time because it is now about three hundred miles long.)

As soon as I settled on this idea for an adventure, my "friends" started asking me pointed questions. I wasn't sure whether they were attempting to test my resolve or talk me out of this crazy-ass idea. Perhaps it was the latter and they were smarter than me.

Every single person whom I made the mistake of telling I was going to hike for two weeks in Minnesota asked: "Minnesota? Why would you go all the way to Minnesota to hike for two weeks when we have lots of perfectly good hiking trails right here?"

Answer: "Because I have never been there...and it sounds nice. I mean, how difficult can it be? It's the Midwest. Isn't it all flat and covered with pretty trees? I can't wait to try something new...and they have all these designated campsites, so I am sure I will find lots of other amazing people to hike with who will become lifelong friends. Oh, I do have my concerns, like why did the guidebook say only seventy people thru-hike the trail every year?"

When I spoke to the few people I ran into who had actually hiked in Minnesota, they all had something else to tell me: it's beautiful, but the bugs. They are everywhere and anywhere. Thick as clouds. Omnipresent. Unstoppable. You will be hating life. Ah, OK. That sounds good. Meanwhile, how come bugs are given such short shrift in the guidebooks? They don't even talk about them. Are the folks in Minnesota just used to them? Is there some sort of innate characteristic in the stoic Scandinavian heritage of the Minnesota soul that does not allow them to complain about bugs? Ya, sure, you betcha.

At an Earth Day event at Lake Tahoe, I began a conversation with a smiling young woman from Minnesota who had just begun working for the Tahoe Rim Trail Association. Her bubbly optimism continued until I asked her about the bugs in Minnesota. Her face quickly contorted to a frown, she shook her head quickly with a definite "No!," and said, "Bring lots of bug spray, wear a net, cover every inch of your body every minute of the day, and perhaps they won't drive you totally bonkers." A few months later, on a hike I was leading, a woman who had been out of Minnesota for many years responded when I told her about the hike: "Oh, my God. The bugs. Bring lots of bug spray."

I was becoming afraid to tell people where I was going because it was inevitable that "bug" would be the first word out of their mouth. A woman on another hike summed up the situation, "Well, you know, everybody in Minnesota leaves the state during the summer to get away from the bugs. They have to or they would go stark raving mad."

But at some point, you have to tell yourself it is not about the bugs…and how bad can they really be that late in the season…(scary drum roll, please). Apparently, they can be really, really bad. Perhaps that is why Minnesotans have a reputation for being quiet and stoic. They know that if they opened their mouths, the bugs would fly in.

In June, two months before departure, I finally launched into full-scale prep mode. I was concerned about the complicated logistics of going halfway across the country to hike. Will it be beautiful or dreary? Will I spend days walking in the freezing rain? Will it be so hot and clammy that it will be like that nightmare of a day I had in June in Charleston, South Carolina? The day when I felt like I was hiking in a steam bath wearing black leather pants? By the time I was done, my thighs were so badly chafed that they looked like a couple of rare steaks rubbing up against each other. I ended up doing a gosh-darn good bowlegged cowboy impression to keep those painful steak thighs from touching each other.

Whatever Minnesota dished out, I consoled myself, it would be different. Every step along the way would lead me to a place I had never been and most likely would never see again. There was a lot to consider, a lot to plan, and now would have been a great time to get to it. But then I thought, "Nah…it can wait."

■ ■ ■

In July, I headed to Muskoka Lakes in Ontario, Canada, for a week to visit my family. I hadn't dealt with food, planned for a shuttle, sent my food drops, or made hotel reservations in Minneapolis. All that can be done in the last few weeks, right? I wasn't even sure how long it would take to hike it. If I averaged about fourteen miles per day with no layover days it would take me seventeen days, making it the longest trip I'd ever done. If the TRT taught me anything, it is that once you are on the trail you are focused on getting to the end. Will it be different in a place I have never hiked? Will a layover day be wanted and needed? Why does backpacking seem so different when you go to a place with which you are not familiar? Will being alone force me to meet more people, and what sort of people will I meet? Why do I waste so much time asking inane questions instead of getting off my butt and getting organized?

I was also experiencing a wave of procrastination with my writing assignments. I heard about a computer program called Write or Die that I thought might be effective. With this program, if you stop plunking away at the keys for more than a few seconds, the screen goes blank and blood slowly dribbles down in front of you, eventually covering up the screen, followed by the sound of screaming babies pleading for mercy. Supposedly, you will then start frantically typing to save these virtual creatures from a horrible death, because who wants to be a baby killer, even a virtual one? Could I use the fear of baby death to force myself to get ready for the trip, or will it only make me write this sentence instead of getting up and checking what is in the refrigerator?

Another method of preparation avoidance was to spend hours reading and rereading the trail section descriptions. Given my fear of heights, I paid particular attention to the notations regarding concerns about children along cliff edges and the dangers of walking across beaver dams. Having never walked across a beaver dam, it sounded intimidating. But how high can it be? I mean, it's built by beavers, so it should be less than twenty feet high, right? There is no such thing as a hike that doesn't scare me, I suppose. Is it the trails or me?

Just five days before departure for Minnesota, I was finally almost ready. I was aware that my pack, like on every other trip I'd ever taken, would be much too heavy. And yet, I would still surely forget something that was absolutely essential. At least I was at that state where you can convince yourself that you are close to being prepared, compared to that nerve-wracking state of spinning in circles because you don't even know where to start. I even survived my scary encounter with what at first glance seemed like the charming small town of Finland, Minnesota. I was online gathering information on Finland, seeing if it might be a suitable location for a food drop, when I read about an eight-year-old boy from the town who had been mauled by a bear. In that same small town, three guys had been recently arrested for accosting canoeists in the Boundary Waters Canoe Area adjacent to the Superior Hiking Trail.

Over the next few days, as I reviewed my list a few times a day, something inane, but seemingly important, would always pop up: will I need nail clippers? What if I cut my nails just before I leave so I get away without clipping them for three weeks? Now, toenails take longer to grow than fingernails, and what does that mean? My seventeenth law of hikeodynamics says, "When life becomes more simple, the few things left that you have to worry about become something that you really worry about." And of course, the regular, totally boring essentials of life take on new meaning if you don't have them with you. While Minnesota is part of the United States, I don't know what it is like there. It just might be the state that just says no to nail clippers.

You can never be too prepared. Just think for a minute about this nightmare: leaving on your two-week trip without lip balm. Every day as you hike in the sunshine, your lips keep getting more chapped. The constant licking only makes it worse. What did cavemen do for their chapped lips? Did they go kill an animal so they could rub its fat all over their face and lips? I bet they couldn't just run to the Flintstone's Corner Pharmacy and pick up a tube of Charlie the Caveman's Squirrel Fat Lip Balm. It's no wonder they all look so glum in those museum dioramas…they have spent their entire lives with chapped lips, long toenails, longer fingernails, and teeth that needed bushing. So kissing might have been a challenge. Or toilet paper! I bet they didn't have even a sheet of toilet paper. Poor guys. Probably wish they didn't have a sense of smell.

Missing that essential item has always been my backpacking nightmare: two weeks without toothpaste, toilet paper, a spoon, or my iPod. OK, at first glance, the lack of an iPod is not something that should elicit insanity, but when hiking alone it can be the difference between keeping it together and an inexorable slow march into craziness. In addition, for appearances sake, if you happen to be walking down a trail singing at the top of your lungs, the wires dangling from your ears should be enough for your fellow hiker to think you are just a happy guy grooving to the tunes. On the other hand, if you are strolling through the woods without a dangling wire in sight, while loudly babbling what sounds like gibberish to the uninformed observer, your fellow hikers may question your sanity. Perhaps they will think you are that crazy guy from whom I ran away a few years earlier on the John Muir Trail.

■ ■ ■

Two days before departure, I checked an online forum about Superior Hiking Trail for the latest conditions. Hikers said that the trail is very dry. In some places where normally copious amounts of water flow, nary a drop can be found. They said the bugs are really bad on the north part of the trail—right where I'm beginning my hike—and that hikers should take all necessary precautions. I loaded up my pack, and, except for the water and electronic stuff, everything was in there. But it was way too heavy. What happened to my great plans for keeping my pack weight down? They scared me with proclamations regarding the lack of water, so I brought an extra water bottle. But after picking up the pack, I took it back out. Then I had an iPod and solar charger and cell phone and camera. Perhaps a wee bit too much food. I didn't have any idea how warm or cold it really gets, so I had a lot of clothes, including rain gear, because when I'm hiking, it rains. Then all the other flotsam and jetsam that eventually add up to real poundage. I've been on dozens of backpacking trips, and every time I have whined about carrying too much weight, and what do I do on my next trip? Whine about carrying too much weight, while doing nothing about it. Backpacking is all about upholding tradition.

DAY ONE
August 22. 7 miles today, 228 miles to go.
Other hikers encountered: 0

My cousin Cindi, whom I'd only met briefly many years earlier, gave me a ride from Minneapolis to her home in Duluth about three hours north. She put me up for the night and rose early the next morning to drive me across the state to the trailhead. There is nothing quite like Midwestern hospitality. It's done with little fuss, and they don't look for acknowledgement. It's just what they believe is the right thing to do, but it really touched my heart to have someone looking after me. Because as you can see by now, I do need looking after.

On the drive north, we passed rocky promontories, swiftly moving streams, and small villages tucked up against the endless blue expanse of Lake Superior. It was glorious country, and I was getting excited for what I knew had to be a grand hiking adventure through spectacular terrain. Then, the pavement ended, and we began a twenty-mile drive on windy, dirt roads through an unending tunnel of deep, dark forest. There were no longer quaint villages, lovely creeks, and stunning rock formations, just a ubiquitous northern forest. Eventually, the road came to an abrupt end at a recently logged opening in the vast forest, where, with absolutely no fanfare, the trail began.

Cindi looked warily around and smiled weakly while taking a picture of me in front of the "This is the start of the Superior Hiking Trail…all who enter beware" sign, or at least in hindsight that is what I believe it should have said. I started walking and Cindi drove away, leaving me all alone in the middle of nowhere. No, really, I know people always talk about being alone in the middle of nowhere, but this really did feel like the absolute middle of nowhere. In fact, it was probably on the other side of the middle of nowhere, which makes the middle of nowhere seem positively civilized.

* * *

After less than a mile of walking, I stopped, looked up toward the sky and screamed, "Holy shit! This is a lot harder than I expected!" It really wasn't a trail; it was more of a vague guideline. An almost impenetrable wall of thick vegetation, with a somewhat softer middle where the branches and deep grass were a little easier to barge through. I used my poles like machetes trying to power through the mess of vines and thick jungle, but I was wishing they had sharp edges to really do the job. In a few places, the greenery wasn't as deep, but you still couldn't see the "trail" underneath your feet because of the giant, slippery roots, rocks, and deep, slimy, wet grass. "Oh, Tahoe Rim Trail…I miss you so…"

It was about this time that I realized the acronym for Superior Hiking Trail (SHT) was in need of an "I" in the middle.

Once in a while, the "trail" would dive into the thick, shady forest and for an oh-such-a-brief period you could actually see the ground. I would stop, gasp for breath, then head onward down a precipitously steep and rocky face, followed immediately thereafter by a nearly impossible-to-maneuver steep and rocky climb through more thick, jungle-like, forest. There were no vistas, no flat sections, just a thick mass of trees, covered in deep tangles of vines, and lots of hot, humid, oppressive air. The air is dry and thin in the Sierra, and oxygen for the unaccustomed can seem to be in short supply. Here in the Midwest, it was as if there were too much oxygen.

As I walked, my brain, in some sort of reverse meditation, kept screaming the mantra, "What in the hell have I got myself into? What in the hell have I gotten myself into?" Since there wasn't another soul within miles, it was OK if I screamed it out loud…because nobody could hear me. In fact, it was a requirement to retain my sanity.

While thick and green and omnipresent, the Minnesota woods were not quiet. The wind roared through the tightly packed trees, creating a fingernails-on-the-chalkboard sound as the trees rubbed together. That competed on the sound meter against the high-pitched chirping of red squirrels that seemed to be hanging out in every tree. There was, however, one piece of good news. While the mosquitoes were certainly bad enough to require repellent, the strong wind made them somewhat bearable.

In a few scattered locations, a bit of gooey mud replaced thick greenery, and I could see hoofprints of moose, along with their scat, but I didn't see any moose. Of course, since the forest was so thick and I was leaning forward, head down, just trying to keep moving and not flip over backward, Bullwinkle could have been twenty feet away and I would have just walked right by without seeing a thing. That and I was mumbling and swearing like a pirate. I just hoped that Indiana Jones was going to arrive any second now and get me out of this mess.

After what felt like about thirty miles of walking but unfortunately was only five, I found myself on the next of many precipitous descents down slippery rock. To keep from rolling down the hill, I placed my hiking poles in front of me and gingerly worked my way down the drop. Just at the steepest point, a bug landed on my leg. As I went to brush it off, I was nearly knocked off my feet by a sharp, ferocious sting. "What the fong goo? That hurts!" I screamed. Instantly, a hefty red mark began swelling painfully. I didn't go into anaphylactic shock, because I am writing this sentence on a computer in Lake Tahoe and not decomposing on the trail. Although given the man-eating jungle through which I was walking, I imagine my decomposition would have occurred so fast it would look like one of those time-lapsed body disintegration scenes on the show *Bones*. But it did create a giant red lump on the side of my leg, which for the rest of the day felt like it was attached to a wire shooting out zaps of pain.

Amid all the fear, loathing, and bug-induced pain, I did graze my way through heaps of ripe thimbleberries and plumb and juicy raspberries. When I stopped to catch my breath in one of those rare, small clearings where the jungle was held briefly at bay, the thick stands of white paper birch and aspen shone brightly white in the sunshine.

Eventually, I made it to the designated campsite. As with most things on this trail, it was not at all what I expected. The campsite consisted of a few boards nailed together about a foot off the ground, which created a narrow platform to place your pack on, a firepit, a small clearing in the thick forest, and a narrow, overgrown pathway to an open-air latrine.

I immediately declared the latrine as the highlight of my day. Set out in a small clearing, at the end of the pathway, it was merely a toilet seat placed on rocks over a hole in the ground. But from there, you can sit and enjoy the forest view. It's a pretty relaxing way to do the morning or evening doo-doo duties. And since there was no one here at camp, it was a pretty safe bet that I could sit in privacy and comfort...for hours, or days, for that matter. I was beginning to think I would have no problem finding privacy on this whole freaking trail. "What other idiot would brave this? Whose lame-brained idea was it to hike this trail? When I get my hands on that thru-hikers' guide author, I tell you..."

True to reports, once I had spent thirty seconds to thoroughly inspect the campsite, I discovered that finding water was going to be an issue. The campsite sat just above a meadow area, and it looked like a fairly respectable creek would normally be going through it. But Minnesota was in a drought, and this creek was now just a bit of oozy mud in the midst of a pile of boulders. I flailed around for a few minutes scrunching my way down into a teensy gap between the boulders where a bit of water trickled up out of the ground into a small, dank pool. Here, I filtered a couple of dirty quarts while frequently batting away the flies and mosquitoes that were attacking my face. Back at camp, just as I began to seriously consider falling into a poor pitiful me melancholy, the rain began to fall. I scurried around, covering packs and putting up rain flies. As is customary, just as I finished my efforts, the rain stopped, and then started up again.

That first night sitting in my tent, I listened to the soft pitter-patter of rain, and wrote:

OK, Rule No.1. Quit feeling sorry for yourself. Sure, it would be nice if my pack were lighter and the trail easier. It would be great if it had some views, if I had water, and if I had a perfect hiking companion. But it is what it is: I can hike my speed, sleep when I want, and do exactly what I want. So buck up, bucko. Walk, eat, poop, pee, sleep, read, write, listen to iPod, repeat as needed. Once you hit the trail, backpacking is quite simple.

I've said before the definition of insanity is doing the same thing over and over again and expecting a different result. Apparently, I did not read my Tahoe Rim Trail thru-hike notes before I planned this adventure. Did I decide that even though I was lonely there in my backyard, in a place where I can practically see my house, that if I flew halfway across the country and went to a place that I'd never been, everything would be wonderful and I would no longer be lonely?

What something is and how one responds to it are different things. Would I revel in the solitude while calmly enjoying the sound of the wind roaring through the white birch trees? Or would I let sadness needle its way into my heart? Unfortunately, on Day One, I went for the latter. I missed my kids. (They may not have missed me and if I were there, would I be fully enjoying them or would they do what teenage daughters do: drive me crazy?) I was not sure if absence made the heart grow fonder, but it does remind you to focus on what is important once you return.

Perhaps instead of being mad at myself for being sad, I needed to understand better what causes my sadness. While I'm one who loves my solitude and time alone, I also enjoy conversing with other humans because they might express different points of view than the pesky, little voices in my head. And if truth be told, I've always been one who needs to hear a second opinion or even a third before I take an important action. When you are the fifth child, you don't naturally assume that you know all the answers. So when I'm alone in the dark in my tent and ponder what would happen at that moment if I had an appendicitis, or a rainstorm carried my tent away, or hear a sound and think, "Wait, was that a bear?" my stomach churns and my head spins because no one else is there to consult. The answers, by the way, to the fears rattling around in my head: I would die, the tent will not fly away because I'm heavy enough to hold it down, and it was just the wind, this time…. Not bad. Based on this I have a 66 percent chance of surviving the evening.

It's all a dilemma. I can't hike by myself because I get lonely, and I can't hike with others, because they get on my nerves and I like to be in control.

Meanwhile, as I contemplated this in my tent, all those tucked-in-tight, white birch trees were rubbing against each other frantically in a wind-crazed orgy, creating a cacophony of screeching sounds like the world's worst horror movie soundtrack.

DAY TWO

August 23. 13 miles today, 20 miles completed, 215 to go. Other hikers encountered: 0

I woke up on Day Two with new resolve to put more miles under my belt. To finish in seventeen days, I needed to average fourteen miles a day, and with only seven completed on Day One, I needed to pick up the pace. I was on the trail by 7:30 a.m. and soon was climbing out of the trees and on to a rocky ridge where there before me, finally, was Lake Superior. It stretched out beyond the horizon. A seemingly endless body of light-blue, utterly still water. Offshore, I could just make out Isle Royale National Park, which for some reason is part of Michigan, the rest of which is located a long way away. The park is a haven for wolves and moose. But its true claim to fame is that allegedly a seasonal pond named Moose Flats, with Moose Boulder in its center, sits in the middle of an island on the largest lake that is located on Isle Royale Island. Thus Moose Boulder becomes "the largest island in the largest lake on the largest island in the largest lake on the largest island in the largest lake in the United States."

Apparently, somebody keeps track of crap like that. And even more astounding, other people have been known to include that trivia in a book. But hold on a sec, it gets more obtuse. National Public Radio and Atlas Obscura.com actually did a story in 2020 on how a mother and a son went out to Isle Royale in search of said Moose Boulder and couldn't find it. Isle Royale, like this bloody Superior Hiking Trail, is remote, thickly forested, and only accessible via boat or plane. It's an all-around pain in the butt to get around, so it makes sense that they couldn't find Moose Boulder before they ran out of time and had to catch a seaplane back to the world. Anyone can investigate the mystery of whether the boulder exists. Before you make your plans, read the rest of this chapter and decide whether tromping through the thick northern jungle is a good idea.

Of course, none of that meant jack to me because I was on the mainland, and Moose Boulder or Moose Poop Lake or whatever was not a place I was going to be soon. I did, however, feel a moment of rejuvenation and relief. I had actually not been transported to another planet that was composed entirely of a dense forest where you could never see more than twenty feet away. I could now see wide-open views of places in the distance that people could find on maps and read inane facts about on Wikipedia.

That said, there is no doubt about it: I was not just hallucinating yesterday; this is a very difficult hike. You can't look up from your feet for more than a second because the path alternates between a slippery, uneven slope to rocky and overgrown with toe-stubbing roots. And sometimes you can have all that challenging stuff at the same time. Almost never did I find lengthy sections of flat and easy walking on soft, sandy trail. The ascents and descents, while often short, were so steep they were barely navigable with a heavy backpack. A plethora of downed trees covering the trail always seemed to be at just the wrong spot on some cliff edge or deep forest. When you are hiking in the Sierra, there is almost always plenty of room just to walk off the trail and around the offending tree. Here, if you head off into the woods, there might be a dozen other downed trees to surmount, so a quick break to get over a tree becomes a lengthy adventure.

As I was just pushing on from my Superior view, a chorus of yipping and howling started in the valley below. This Sierra Nevada resident immediately thought it must be coyotes, but this sound was deeper, more resonant. Wolves. It was an incredibly powerful and touching sound of pure wildness. It spoke of lonely northern woods, of long, tough winters, of a time gone by when the sound of wolves was a backdrop to a difficult adventure in the backcountry. It made me want to grow my beard, lose a tooth or two, and move the can of beans roasting on the flames with a big set of tongs before I spat into the fire.

Back in the northern Minnesota forest, the trail was a marvel of teeming life. Thimbleberries were ripe, juicy, and tasty. Frogs, which provided a steady chorus of croaking, remained invisible on perfectly matching foliage until they went for a hop. Every tree was covered in moss or had a rainbow of mushrooms at its base. It was like walking inside a giant terrarium where some interesting clump of greenery was packed into every cubic inch.

If you look closely, a dense forest is like a city. Not a well-organized or well-planned city, but a chaotic, crowded urban metropolis. Spiders throw out webs over here, a squirrel rummages through a pile of cones over there. Plants climb on top of each other to find that piece of dirt, a bit of water, a place in the sun. The tallest trees are the office skyscrapers, packed with squirrels and birds dwelling in the heights. The shrubs and younger trees are the medium-size apartment buildings. Closer to the ground are the busy city streets, where wildflowers and grasses, like stores, attract the pollinators, the buzzing bees, and hummingbirds. Under the ground is the subway, where moles and gophers have created tunnels for water to move from place to place to feed the grass that feeds the mice that feed the birds that feed the coyotes. Other mammals cruise through the complicated maze picking off the weakest, the slowest, or just those with bad luck or timing. Countless different niches and occupations live on top of each other. All frantically work to grow and build their own dream, which is to survive to make more of what they are.

■ ■ ■

By midafternoon I made it to Carlson Pond, a large beaver pond, where I filled up with enough water to get me through the night since the campsite was three miles farther and had no water. The Hazel Campsite was a delightful clearing in a cheery grove of aspen and birch, with matted grasses on which you could lie down and see the sky! For me, "lie down" meant "collapsing." It was warm and pleasant being down on the ground and not moving, but my thoughts again turned to wonderment about why I'm doing this. In the back of my mind, I knew I would be lonely and that the hiking would be hard. But the front of my mind tried to pooh-pooh the back of my mind, saying to be lonely was just a sign of weakness. I should be able to hunker down and power through it. I've been a backpacker for decades. I wrote two guidebooks about hiking, one of which is about backpacking with kids. How could I let a feeling of loneliness get to me on the trail?

I think we all have the ability to have selective memory with our travel experiences. I remembered the good parts of that Tahoe Rim Trail trip, but shunted aside the feelings of loneliness that often curled their way into my belly once I arrived at camp. Now I found myself on this bus that I couldn't get off for at least another fourteen days, and I had to work my way through the hollow feelings and keep on walking.

I looked forward to tomorrow when, according to what I read, I would be at a creek into which I could actually wade. I would walk into a state park, and perhaps I would actually see and have the opportunity to talk to a fellow human being. The day after that, I was scheduled to stroll along the shore of Lake Superior.

On Day Two, however, I spent the day without seeing another person. Normally during the day, you talk to people and your brain revolves around those conversations. My brain was revolving around the conversations I was having with myself. We talked about the wind, or the temperature, or how far I had to go to reach this point or that. But mostly my brain was talking about the pain, how the pack was hurting my shoulders, and how that nasty rash that formed where the pack meets my back was beginning to form blisters, which I could feel, but couldn't see. My body was unaccustomed to hiking in humidity. While it only hurt when I took a step, unfortunately that is a requirement for walking long distances. But sometimes, when my mind was focused on the music in my head, I would be cruising along thinking about nothing, just walking, and very, very slowly, watching the miles go by…then my brain would say, "Hey, this is great, I'm not thinking about pain anymore," which of course would make it think about pain again. And what I am not sure of is whether any of those thoughts might have actually emerged through my mouth, but who gives a rat's ass since there was no one there to hear them!

If you are going to spend evenings by yourself in the middle of nowhere, it's always cool to have maps and a guidebook. After reading the apropos book chapter several times and looking at one map, you can study the other map (which is almost identical) and continue the never-ending conversation: "If I went to this campsite tomorrow, then the next day I could make it to here. But if I go to this other campsite farther, perhaps I could make it to that other campsite the next day." By the second day, I was already calculating how to increase the average daily mileage to get me off the trail a day sooner. But the problem was I did thirteen miles on Day Two and afterward could hardly walk. There was no way I could keep up this pace for another fifteen days. The other option of course was the one I tried not to think about: screw it, hike my own pace, and when I am done, call Cindi to rescue me somewhere. In addition to the embarrassment of having to tell my cousin that I failed, I felt that I'd worked too hard and planned the trip too long to give up. The final question for my evening was: it's Saturday night in August, and I did not see a person all day long. Does anybody else know this trail exists?

DAY THREE

**August 24. 12 miles today, 32 completed, 203 miles to go.
Average: 10.6 miles per day. Other backpackers encountered: 0.
Park peepers: A few**

I spent the morning wielding hiking poles like machetes, slashing viciously through shrubbery, hoping that I was still on the pathway. I passed several of the now-familiar teensy, weensy creeks that were supposed to be places for me to douse myself in cool, clear water. They were not enticing for a swim, and a good piss would double their flow. I assuaged the pain by gorging on thimbleberries before crossing a major dirt road where the world changed.

Now I could actually see dirt under my feet and feel for the first time on this trip that I was on a hiking trail—one perhaps used by other people. A few miles later, I heard the enchanting sound of swiftly running water, and then suddenly, there it was. Close enough to touch. The Brule River in Judge C. R. Magney State Park: seventy-five feet across, babbling, bustling, and beautiful. I immersed myself in her cool, clear waters. While the chilly water cleansed and refreshed my soul, the sunshine warmed my heart. A brief moment of bliss. A reason to continue this infernal hike. Once again, backpacking revealed both its dirty dark secret and the reason we keep coming back for more: the power of relativity. Backpacking teaches you to truly enjoy the simple joys of a quick dip in a mountain stream by ensuring you had several days of brutish, hellish nightmare preceding it.

■ ■ ■

After my swim, the trail wandered along the cheery stream, which babbled its way toward the locally famous Devil's Kettle Falls. For the first time in three days, I heard a strange sound…voices…human voices. I was soon surrounded by several large, blond, untanned Minnesotans followed shortly thereafter by the roaring root beer float that is the falls. While you might guess that the idea for the abominable snowman came from explorers trudging across the frozen Arctic, I believe it came from someone the first time they saw a pale, humongous, white Minnesotan not wearing a shirt. The only thing whiter is snow, and that would just be the fresh, powdery variety.

A large rock splits Devil's Kettle Falls into two branches. The main channel is a wide wave of froth plunging into a deep pool. The other branch also shoots a voluminous quantity of water roaring toward the pool, but all that water disappears into a hole in the rock known as the Devil's Kettle. I kept looking downstream without any luck trying to see where that massive quantity of missing water reappeared. Apparently, I'm not alone in my curiosity. In efforts to solve the mystery over the years, folks have thrown boxes of ping-pong balls, logs, and other detritus into the kettle. But all their efforts were for naught because not even one of those ping-pong balls ever popped back up. They must be still down there somewhere spinning around like they are stuck in a washing machine.

After musing about Devil's dilemma for more time than it warranted, I started walking again and soon was out of the park, not to see another human for the rest of the day. I walked right past people at the falls but never spoke a word. Did I lose my ability to speak, or did the reserved ambience of the local population keep me from speaking to strangers? Perhaps we were all just too puzzled with life's important questions like: where the hell did that water go?

Does anybody actually camp on the Superior Hiking Trail? In three days of hiking, I'd seen one other hiker. At the falls, I did see some of the carry-a-bottle-and-bring-the-toddlers crowd, but it seems to be a hiking trail without actual hikers. Well, the guidebook author did say only seventy people thru-hike the trail each year. Sounds like that might be an exaggeration. Not that a guidebook author would ever do that.

Just after Kettle Falls, lengthy, very steep stairs that would take the bluster out of anyone's sails quickly eliminated the folks who were just out for a stroll. It was certainly a motivation buster for me, and all the fun times I'd had at the Brule River quickly faded away. The trail eventually topped out, was well maintained, and became a pleasant walk. Much of the trail was a wide, mowed grass lane, used as a cross-country ski trail in the winter. I kept walking past the first two Little Brule River campsites to reach the farthest and, unfortunately, by far the least desirable campsite of the three.

When they decided to name this river the Little Brule River, the accent was very much on the little. It wasn't really running, but only popped up now and then from the muddy bed. The last Little Brule River campsite had no flat spots and only very steep access to the nonexistent creek. So I tromped back almost a half mile to the other two spots.

Wait, wait. That can't be right. Did I actually proclaim that I turned around to walk back in the direction from whence I'd come? Breaking the cardinal rule of thru-hikers? Backtrack? It just isn't done. Hiking back almost a half mile means adding almost a mile to the total distance of my hike. Committing this atrocious act would certainly lead to my ostracism at the imaginary thru-hiker meetings, but this was one of those rare occasions when it was worth going backward. My new campsite was a delightful spot in a flat, grassy grove of aspens. Instead of difficult access to the nonexistent river, this one had easy access to the nonexistent river. I ambled over to the parched riverbed, searching for a trickle of running water, and eventually found a yard-square hole where a bit of water percolated to the surface. A few tiny fish listlessly swam in the tiny bit of dank water. It looked like an advertisement for why you need a water filter.

I nearly drained the pool with my measly half gallon of water then had time to ponder the forest of the northern Midwest. Life here in the summer is just falling all over each other to happen. White birch, beech, spruce, aspen, and cedar are packed in so tightly it's hard to imagine another tree finding a spot. Trees so thick, if it were not for the trail, walking would be impossible. Below the trees, the tiniest piece of dirt is immediately occupied by something green, thick, and bubbling with life that grows like crazy. And then there are the ubiquitous squirrels chirping loudly and incessantly, birds of every type imaginable, as well as snakes and frogs and bugs and fish and everything else that nature can throw out there to occupy any unoccupied space. Where there is an opening for a stream, a blue heron probably floats above the shore. If you are strolling along a ridgeline, hawks, eagles, and vultures are surely gliding above your head. Mostly, to love these forests, you have to love green, because every shade and contour of green is represented, which makes the stark whiteness of the paper birch bark stand out like a large, untanned, rural Minnesotan without a shirt.

■   ■   ■

As I tried to comfort my sore muscles that evening, I heard loud pecking and crunching noises that I first thought must be a tree being ripped apart by a bear, and a big one. Then, filtered through the trees, I could see first one enormous red head and then a second one. Two pileated woodpeckers were attacking some unfortunate birch tree. Woodpeckers, so enormous and so clownishly colored that at first glance it was hard to believe they were real.

Although I hadn't seen anyone on the trail since Devil's Kettle Falls, I could hear a dog barking and the sounds of an ATV revving somewhere in the distance. This trail is schizophrenic. There are no hikers on the trail, but I get the sense that just outside of view there is a network of dirt roads bringing folks to their remote, rustic cabins in the deep woods. Cue the *Deliverance* music.

Later, sitting in camp waiting for the sun to go down, I once again fell prey to unfathomable pangs of loneliness. Maybe it was the sound of dogs and humans that reminded me that I am alone while others are making connections. A part of me was trying to convince myself that this was my chance to do this trip. I'd invested time and energy to take on this challenge. I should embrace it and revel in accomplishing a tough goal.

As the yogi woo-woos would say, I need to live in the present, which I was frequently reminding myself to do. Another part of me was sad because life is short and we cannot accomplish it all, and the real bummer is that we cannot be in two places at once. This trip was something I felt I needed to be doing, but I also needed to be spending the last precious weeks with my daughter Sarah before she headed off to college. I understood that I had chosen to ride this bus with no one else on it in the midst of the northern Minnesota wilderness. A part of me just wanted to yank the cord and tell the driver to let me off; another part was determined to continue, because otherwise I would feel as if I were a failure.

DAY FOUR

August 25. 14 miles today, 46 completed.
189 miles to go. Average: 11.5 miles per day

I was stoked. I was about to compete in my first cross-country ski race of the year, and then I realized that I was not wearing any clothes. I called my daughter in a panic, pleading, "Can you meet me at the start in Portland with my ski clothes?"

"Dad, wait, Portland? Do they even get snow?"

In the next image, my teeth were chattering as I shivered through blinding snow and sleet, gliding up a steep hill in a crowd of skiers, many snickering as I skied past. I looked down and noticed that I was wearing tight spandex bike shorts and a brightly colored short-sleeved bike jersey. And nothing else. Then I woke up. Still in the warm woods of Minnesota. Still on the thru-hike bus.

I attempted to move and realized that shivering in my bike shorts in the snow would be less painful. I contorted around to take a gander at the nasty saddle sores where my pack had been rubbing up against the top of my butt cheeks. It looked like someone had taken two pileated woodpecker heads and splatted them onto my back.

I crawled out of my tent to continue my inventory. My hips were moaning, shooting out little messages that said, "Whoa...don't go there," while my shoulders were aching on both the front and backside. My toes expressed absolutely no interest in toe tapping. This was only Day Four. To get my mind off the pain, I rotely packed up and focused on moving, hoping the actions would loosen up my rusty joints.

After a few days on the trail, packing up is a quiet, thought-free, smooth transition: pick up the tent pegs, fold up the tent, boil water for breakfast, create this huge pile ready to be stuffed into the pack. Then it all is packed away out of sight, and you look around and it is as if you were never there. It's like a Tibetan sand painting. The monks gracefully work to create this incredible work of art with different colors of sand and then when they are finished, they sweep it all away. Every evening when they get to camp, backpackers gracefully create their own little world. They quickly decide where is the most comfortable place to sit, the best views, the bathroom spot, and the kitchen. Then the next morning, they smoothly wrap it all up and take it with them to create a new home a few miles away.

Once my home was securely stored inside my backpack, I rambled through the deep woods, and in two miles I stepped onto the edge of a wide expanse of asphalt, Highway 61, the lifeblood of the Minnesota North Shore. I crossed the highway quickly, avoiding the temptation to put out my thumb and hitch a ride back to Duluth, and reached the shore of Lake Superior. The lake was utterly still, impossibly vast, and crystal clear. There was an early-morning calm, stirred only by a couple quietly rustling in their sleeping bags where the beach met the forest. The pebble beach held the world's largest supply of perfect skipping stones. They were piled up several feet thick, forming steep ledges of rocks far up the slope, created by powerful winter storms pummeling the lake. I was in no hurry; the immense lake was mesmerizing. I'd heard people comment on the incredible clarity of my home lake, Lake Tahoe, my whole life, but the utterly clear translucence of this corner of Lake Superior appeared even clearer. I didn't see a whiff of algae or anything else growing on the rocks under the surface.

While several campers and tents were scattered along my mile-and-a-half walk along the lakeshore, I found a sheltered spot behind the rocks, doffed my clothes, and slipped into Superior's magical waters. On that warm August morning, I quickly discovered why the lake was so clear. It was bone-chillingly freakin' cold! Glacial tarn with patches of ice still melting in it cold. October have to get in it, but can hardly stand it cold. Fall in the hole while ice fishing in the middle of the winter cold…well, perhaps not that bad, but definitely really, really cold. I emerged from the water very quickly, clean and ready for the day. Well, as clean as you can be when you get in the water, attempt to breathe again, then get the hell out as fast as you possibly can.

Along the shore, the sun slowly warmed away the shivers. I thought that a better plan than hiking for the next thirteen days would be to set up my tent at the bluff above the lake and just hang out here. I could sit next to my tent and write wonderful passages about the beauty of this immense lake. Then every day or two, I would develop enough nerve to get back into the frosty water to rinse off. But alas, eventually I groaned, got up, and began walking away from the lake. I had a trail to finish. It's what thru-hikers do.

I crossed the highway again and headed into the woods. The good news was that the ice bath had cooled some of the fire on my aching muscles. The bad news was that after the level lakeshore, my route set off on a sustained climb to the Kadunce River. Except for the walk along the lake, these Minnesota root beer rivers are the highlights of the trip. By the time water reaches the rivers and streams of Minnesota, it has filtered through bogs or swamps loaded with minerals. These minerals give the water a root beer–brown color that at first makes you feel that the water is dirty, but you soon get used to that just being the color of water in the forested north. When the water goes over a falls or a steep cascade, it adds foam for the full root beer–float effect.

After the Kadunce, I took a dip in Kimball Creek. It was just a half mile from the trailhead on a major dirt road, but I felt pretty comfortable I could skinny-dip here in privacy. I had discovered that unless you are standing at the base of a waterfall to which someone can push a stroller, you can be assured of having this trail to yourself.

Two swims made Day Four a good day, but a very long one. Every once in a while as I was walking, my hip would send out a sharp pain and loudly proclaim, "Yo, Tim, you can stop right here, I'm not planning on walking anymore." I would come to a screeching halt, twist my leg a few times, and then tentatively take a few steps. The pain would go away, only to snap me again like a well-placed locker room towel a half hour later. By the time I got to camp, I was so stiff and sore that I couldn't sit in one place for too long. That was when I realized that if finishing this makes me a real mountain man, perhaps I am not a real mountain man. There must be an easier way for me to gain my credentials.

At about seven o'clock in the evening, I was reading in my tent, trying hard not to move because every movement would induce some sort of sharp pain, when I heard a crashing noise. I tried to get up with my stiff hips, sore legs, and tender shoulders, but then decided it wasn't worth it. I felt like I was the old dog that makes such a mighty struggle to get up to go for a walk that his owner looks at him and sadly proclaims, "I wonder how much longer we can wait before we have to put him down." I relaxed and said, "The hell with it," wondering if someone would come along to put me down soon and end my misery.

■ ■ ■

I did speculate at length whether when I woke up in the morning I would be capable of walking, let alone completing the remaining 189 miles. I thought: when they find my rotting body, which of course might not be for a few years because it would require somebody to actually hike this trail, will they know that I hiked myself to death?

DAY FIVE
August 26. 14 miles today, 60 completed,
175 miles to go. Average 12 miles per day

First off, let me say that with the benefit of hindsight, I can clearly state that this was the worst day of the trip. It had all the fixins for a bad day all neatly packaged for my nonenjoyment. But let's begin with the highlight of the day, which was popping a few luscious thimbleberries off the bushes next to my tent and dumping them into my bowl of cereal. It was all downhill from there, except that it did require a lot of walking uphill.

Along the placid Woods Creek, I listened to the soft gurgling of the water and stared vacantly from my tent at the still-wet clothes hanging on the line. It was warm and sunny the day before, so it seemed like a perfectly logical time to wash my clothes. I set up a clothesline in the sun and waited for them to dry, and waited and waited, thinking for sure they would be dry before I went to bed. Lesson No. 1 for hiking in humid environments: things never dry.

Like the day before, my hips were so sore and stiff that it was a struggle to get up. I threw my pad onto the dirt, slowly plopped out of the tent face first, and at glacial speed rose onto my hands and knees. I did a few Cat-Cow yoga poses, ostensibly to stretch, but more likely a method to delay standing up. One knee at a time with a loud grunt, I finally made it to standing. A quick inventory concluded I might be an old, sore, and tired dog, but I was not quite ready to be put down yet.

I packed up a pile of still-wet clothes, and made a swift descent into the deep, dark canyon of the Devil Track River. That of course led to a steep and relentless climb out of the canyon on a series of precipitous steps. One heavy stride at a time, over and over again, in a seemingly endless climb to the top, with occasional breaks to expel a raspy "What the fuck?" Once I finally made it to the top, things briefly got better as I began walking on cross-country ski trails to the outskirts of Grand Marais, the town designated as my first food resupply. The town is about one-and-a-half miles from the trail, so I decided to hitch a ride into town. A stoic older gentleman who wasn't interested in conversation gave me a quiet ride to town. I was happy not be walking. I did notice that the ride was all downhill, which of course would be important if on the way back up I was unable to garner a ride.

I sat on the grass next to the Grand Marais post office after picking up my food resupply package, and I haphazardly tossed a big pile of clothes and food on the lawn trying to figure out how in the hell all of it was going to fit in my pack. The locals on their way to pick up the mail took a glance and saw a guy in dirty clothes making a mess on their town lawn and gave me pinched "What has the world come to?" looks. They were polite of course, this is the Midwest, but I clearly felt they were dubious of this backpack-wearing outsider in their charming, little town. Don't they know that there is this two-hundred-mile-long hiking trail a mile from town? Oh, yeah, now I remember, the Superior Hiking Trail is in some sort of space-time-*Twilight Zone* continuum. Nobody actually knows that it exists.

Eventually, after several choice swear words and some perfectly good supplies summarily pitched into the garbage, I realized that I could not possibly stuff anything more into my pack. Then I attempted to pick it up and realized that it was too damn heavy. And that was before I lumbered on down to the market to pick up a few perishables.

After five days on the trail, a market is a place of startling sensory overload: shining red bell peppers, bright-yellow bananas, and vibrant-green vegetables flowing over the top of counters under the bright lights. It smelled like sweet, moist freshness and health. There were cold drinks, ice, and hundreds of little items that we use every day and take for granted until we put on our backpacks and head into the woods and they are no longer available. But I had to pass all that cornucopia of excess and instead get some hard cheese, that damn salami, and of course a few cookies. Oh wait, and a candy bar. Well, just one banana.

Every time I enter a market in the midst of a backpack trip, I'm overwhelmed. Once we don our backpacks, it doesn't take us long to get used to the simple life of living with little on the trail. But then when we return to the well-stocked larders of the civilized world, we are jarred by how much of it there is, and how while we really don't need all that stuff, it still looks pretty damn tasty.

I walked very gingerly up and down the narrow aisles with my gigantic pack, sure that at any moment I would back into a display, knocking over hundreds of cans, which then would lead to a crashing and general tumult similar to what I'd seen in dozens of movies. A loud hubbub would ensue, followed by murmurings of "That's it, let's string him up." And they didn't even know that I am from California. Yet. That would really send them over the edge.

They were polite at the counter, and I'm sure I was just being paranoid, but I thought I saw walking up the aisle the same person who was looking at me suspiciously and rolling their eyes at the post office just a few minutes earlier. Either way, I was continuing to confirm the town's knee-jerk diagnosis of me as a numbskull. Perhaps they are just good judges of character.

When I was in graduate school at Cornell, they called me a "Frisbee-brained Californian" because I had the temerity, on those very rare sunny Upstate New York days, to catch Frisbees flying over the lovely expanse of grass on the campus quad. Why would I want to be cooped up in the library working on my thesis when it was finally beautiful outside? In my two years in Ithaca, I could count the number of blessed, warm, sunny days on my two hands and maybe half a foot. I'd spent countless hours in that damn library, trying to measure up to Ivy League life, but when I look back, it's the time spent watching the disc float gently through the air with McGraw Tower in the background that I hold most dearly.

After escaping from my paranoia and the market, I headed to the diner for a real lunch. Again, people were cautiously friendly, but I certainly felt unwanted when I tromped into the quiet restaurant and plunked my pack down onto the booth seat. And by plunked I mean dropped with a crash, which given the pack's new weight, turned every head in the place in my direction. I'm sure the food was fine, but it was not as exciting as I had dreamed about for the last few days, because I now realized that I didn't belong in this town. I was just wasting potential hiking time getting depressed when I belonged back in the woods doing my job. Getting this trail done.

Before leaving town, however, I realized that this would be a good time to communicate with folks in my world. I stopped in front of the town library and smashed my pack down onto a picnic table in the shade and called home, but no one answered.

Then I called my brother to wish him a happy birthday. He was visiting my parents at their summer home in Canada. Everyone got on the line and began telling me stories about how they were enjoying lovely boat rides on the lake and lounging on the dock. My brother talked about golf games, tennis matches, and how stuffed he was from eating all the delicious food.

The family then proceeded to tell me what an idiot I am for doing this trip. I'm not sure, but this might have been shortly after I did a teeny bit of whining about how everything had not been going as well as I had hoped and that I was sad and lonely and people were not nice to me. My dad summed up the tenor of the conversation when he softly asked a poignant question: "What's the point?"

Um. I used to know what the point was, but now I'm not so sure. At first, the point was to go on a longer trip than the Tahoe Rim Trail to prepare for an even longer trip such as a substantial section of the Pacific Crest Trail, perhaps someday leading to hiking the entire PCT. At the time I was on the phone, I was angry that they were not more supportive of what I was doing, that they just didn't understand why I was doing this, and if they did they would be encouraging me, instead of bringing me down. But later, when I was marching up another steep hill in the infernal heat and had lots of time on my hands to think about it, I began to seriously ask myself my dad's question: "What in the hell is the point? Why am I doing this?"

I really wasn't sure what the point was except to keep walking. And once again, I confirmed what I had learned while hiking the Tahoe Rim Trail: do not call people in the real world during a backpack trip; they will only bring you down. They just don't get it. Besides, I couldn't dillydally. I had just stuffed my pack to the gills with a seven-day supply of food, and I still had about eight more miles of hiking today. So I shouldered up, and bucked up, and began walking out of town.

The problem with getting a ride into town is that you are not really paying attention to the road. Now that lack of attention was coming home to roost, because I really had no idea how to get out of Grand Marais and back to the trailhead. I knew the general direction was up, so I followed one street that I hoped would lead to the right place. It turned out to be a dead end, so I walked back down and started up another street. It didn't take long to realize that trudging up the wrong asphalt road in the afternoon sun was much less enjoyable than sitting on a park bench in the shade. Finally, in a totally un-dad move, I asked for directions and made my way to the Gunflint Trail, a road which I was told would lead me back to the damn SH missing-the-I T. At first, I halfheartedly tried to hitch a ride, but the cars were going so fast and given my reception in town I'd had my fill of folks from Grand Marais, so I just plodded on. Moaning. Sweating. Trudging slowly up the hot tarmac, until after what seemed like forever, but was probably only half of forever, I finally reached the trail. My excitement was quickly doused when I realized that reaching the trail did not mean I would be leaping into a cool lake where naked maidens would fan me with palm fronds. Instead, the trail just continued to head uphill steeply in the hot afternoon sun, just like the road had. And for the first time in five days, it was not a trail inundated with thick vegetation providing much-needed shade. Instead, it was a treeless slope shimmering in the stifling August heat.

As I climbed toward views of Lake Superior, I turned to music to take my mind away from this day. It helped when Loggins and Messina and Led Zeppelin were playing, but then along came the Beatles singing "Eleanor Rigby," asking where the lonely people come from, and where they belong. I now know one place where they come from: Lake Tahoe. And where do they belong? Hell, if I know, but apparently it was not a hiking trail in Minnesota, since there were no people on this trail except me.

Looking back at this day, I wonder what my old Catskill hiking buddy Linda would have said if she saw me on the trail doing all this griping about being alone. "Are you kidding me? You are complaining because there are no other people on the trail?" she would have said. "That is my dream. That is why you go out there. Why would you want to see other people?" She has a good point. There have been many times while hiking I've been disappointed when I see that first other person on the trail. Which of course gets back to why I'm frustrated that I allow myself to be lonely on the trail.

* * *

Eventually, I reached a long, mostly flat section on an old road. It was sizzling, without a lick of water or breath of wind. I even missed the shade of the omnipresent jungle-like forest. I knew I still had lots of monotonous miles to hike before I reached what I was sure would be a dreary campsite. So I kept on keeping on, as you can tell, loaded with boundless optimism and a cheery disposition.

This long, open section through nothingness gave me a chance to realize something that I dearly miss on this trail. Something abundant along the trails of the Sierra: a place to put your pack down. Given the grueling weight of a backpack, it's important to find a spot where you can sit down, take your pack off, and then be able to put it back on and rise up onto your feet. It is often almost impossible to get the behemoth from the ground all the way up onto your shoulders. The best spot is a flat piece of granite about two feet off the ground, and the Sierra is blessed with billions of them. Of course, there is an art to finding the right one. If it is sloped too much to the front, your pack will fall forward, perhaps spilling your contents or smashing something of value inside. This pack-falling ceremony only occurs when you have opened several pockets of the pack and then wandered off to take a leak, since the second law of Packodynamics states that the pack will not start to fall until you are at least far enough away that you cannot run back and save it before it tumbles to the ground. On the other hand, if the slope of the rock leads the pack to lean too far backward, it may go careening over the rear of the rock, somersaulting end over end down a mountainside…which would definitely not be good.

The Superior Hiking Trail is mostly bereft of granite rocks that are excellent for pack removal. While there are lots of trees and many of them have fallen to the earth, they are for the most part spindly things that are too low to the ground and do not accommodate a pack without instant tumbling. So here you just keep on hiking, trudging along for miles with sore shoulders, searching in vain for the perfect pack-removal spot.

The last two paragraphs once again point out that minor issues that wouldn't matter at all to the average observer become paramount to the backpacker. When you are backpacking, the focus is on just the most basic of basics of life, such as finding the perfect place to put your pack down, the perfect place to camp, or the all-important perfect place to poop. Unfortunately, being humans, instead of relishing the simplicity that backpacking affords, we have to make it more complicated. We choose to make everything we think about intense, complex, and of course very important and serious. Snap out of it, you idiot. You are just walking. A very long way. With your whole world on your back.

After more than fifteen miles of walking, counting my funky foray into town, I finally reached the North Bally Creek Pond Campsite. If you are hiking the Superior Hiking Trail and can avoid this campsite, do so. That might be hard to do, however, because the next campsite headed north is more than ten miles away, well past Grant Marais itself. For those such as me headed south toward Cascade Park, it's another five grueling miles to the next site. And I was way too thirsty and tired to walk another five miles. What about the idea of just breaking the rules and camping somewhere along the trail that was not a designated campsite? It just never entered my brain until now as I write this. Well, that wasn't a viable option either because there were no spots with water to camp, but it is an interesting comment on my mindless devotion to following the rules that it never even occurred to me.

The camp sat on a slope that required setting up the tent on an angle that would make sleep difficult. The only view was of the impenetrable brush that surrounded the entire campsite, and the ground was a thick layer of fine brown dust that immediately stuck to everything. Oh, and for the first time in four days, the bugs were absolutely horrific. I didn't have the time or energy to drown in my sorrows, however. I desperately needed to get into water.

Supposedly, water for a much-needed cleansing was to be found at an unseen beaver pond just below the site. I walked down excitedly with my filter and bottles and reached a dried-up meadow that appeared as if at some point in the distant past might have been a fairly large beaver pond. Now, the bottom of the supposed pond was dry, cracked ground. Little bits of vegetation grew in the cracks. Swimming was definitely out, but was there even any water to drink? I wandered around the former water body searching out a remnant, and I finally found a tiny puddle, less than the size of a garage. It teemed with slimy algae and other yucky-looking stuff floating on the top; its deepest and cleanest point reached a depth of about two inches. Two freakin' inches of slime. I carefully lay down on the dirt, gazed into water that I couldn't believe I had to drink, and began filtering. Even after passing through the filter, it produced a chocolate milk-like concoction. Apparently, filtering this stuff was not enough, so I boiled the murky water as well. Having to drink this brown brew was the icing on this interminable and miserable day. Get me the hell outta here!

DAY SIX

August 27. 12 miles today, 72 miles completed, 163 miles to go. Average: 12.0

In the morning, I did have the opportunity to get the hell outta there and headed off on a five-mile jaunt to the Cascade River and its state park. It was a lovely swath of water, wide and strong. A breath of fresh sanity after that hellhole where I had spent the night. I immersed myself in a foot-deep hole and let the water roll over me, trying to reclaim my severely deflated soul.

Rejuvenated, I followed the Cascade River downstream, soon passing an enchanting cascade that bottomed out in a deep, clear pool. It looked like the spot I should have swam in if I had my druthers. It looked like the perfect swimming hole. A hundred yards farther, I met a young hiker who during our brief chat mentioned that he was on his way to a great swimming hole. Yes, I know exactly where it is. That's what happens when you just can't wait any longer: you immerse yourself in whatever piece of delightful water comes your way. But I have been hiking long enough to know that if one waits for the perfect swimming hole, one (and by one, I mean me) usually ends up on the top of some ridge wondering how come I didn't swim in that lovely creek that I walked beside for three miles. It also points out that while striking out and trying new trails expands your mind, there are certainly some enormous advantages to being a local and knowing all the best spots.

The Superior Hiking Trail climbed steeply away from the river onto a ridge then dropped back alongside the river again, just in time to view an incredible series of waterfalls. Torrents of raging brown topped by foamy white heads dropped into big pools before disappearing into a steep gorge.

The problem with rivers and lakes is that water falls to the lowest point. Once you leave the water, you have to go up. I began a hefty climb through a lush forest laden with thimbleberries to a viewpoint at Lookout Mountain. Here, a vast expanse of forest sloped down to the shores of Lake Superior. No wonder it seemed like I had been hiking through an endless forest of tightly packed trees. As far as I could see was an endless forest of trees. A nonstop, leafy, green oxygen machine.

■　■　■

Animal interlude: The Red Squirrel is like other squirrels except with the energy level of a Tour de France racer who just drank twelve cups of coffee. If you look up hyper in the dictionary, the definition should say red squirrel. Not only are they nonstop action, but they are not intimidated by humans and in fact like to get very close before unleashing their jet engine-loud, raucous clamor. They enjoy informing you in no uncertain terms that they are the boss and that you have to listen to them. Now. And in the forests of the Midwest, they are everywhere.

⁎ ⁎ ⁎

Eventually, I ended up at a lovely campsite next to little Indian Camp Creek. As seems to be the theme, it was a very small stream, but at least it was moving and big enough to filter water. As I was happily filtering away next to the creek, a powerful blast of water suddenly splattered my face and shot deep up my nostrils. "Waa, what the hell was that?" I exclaimed. I quickly realized that the hose that emits from the top of the filter had come off just as I was pumping swiftly downward. Stupid Tim trick. Later, in a sure sign of exhaustion, even after repeated efforts, I could not get my stove to start. What could possibly be the problem with this workhorse machine that had always started right up with the first click? Eventually, after a thorough analysis, I discovered the apparent problem. To produce a flame, the stove actually has to be attached to the gas canister. Another Stupid Tim trick.

The clouds rolled in, and a few light drops of rain began pattering down as I tried my phone atop a knoll where I could get reception. I left a message, a plea, for my cousin Cindi: "Hi…I've decided to get out on Day Eight. I can catch a shuttle or hitch a ride, but I wanted to let you know."

⁎ ⁎ ⁎

What a relief! After six days of pressing hard to meet a pace that would allow me to finish on time or even early, I was tired, sore, depressed, and sick of dealing with water issues. And then there was my stomach, which was constantly dishing out a cacophony of growling and gurgling sounds, as well as a good deal of cramping and pain. Apparently, getting your water supply from dung-infested beaver ponds or two-inch-deep mud slicks is not conducive to a happy belly. I'd decided it was time to get back to what backpacking should be about: happily walking through the woods, finding peace in the quiet, and feeling the sun and the wind. I decided that not only would I leave in two days, I would just hike seven miles the next day so I could camp along the shores of Lake Agnes. An actual, honest-to-goodness lake. After arranging for my escape, I sprinted back to camp and dived into my tent just as a light pattering transitioned into a steady rain. In the middle of the night, I was awakened by the crack of thunder, followed shortly by rain pounding so hard it felt like a fire hose blasting the tent. Every few seconds, an impossibly bright light would flash above my head. I would then hold my breath and count the seconds until the crashing thunder violently shook the tent. Now what was that rule again? Number of seconds divided by the reciprocal equals how many quarter miles away the strike is? One of the skills that I wish my mom had not taught us six kids growing up was to have a healthy, or perhaps unhealthy, fear of lightning. I remember many Tahoe summer evenings when my mom would drag all the kids into the hallway where we (more likely she) couldn't see the flashes. She proceeded to frantically treat us to the latest rendition of the story that we had heard every time there was a lightning storm: as an eight-year-old child, she was staying in a Kansas City hotel when lightning struck it. That part didn't change over the years, but with each telling, the strike knocked off a larger and larger chunk of the building. Good thing we grew up and moved away; that poor building and perhaps the rest of the city would have been destroyed by a few more tellings. Her plan to instill a fear of lightning worked—it still scares the shit out of me. I was not overjoyed that night to be prone with white knuckles in that little frame of metal lightning rods as the sound of thunder crashed down around me.

DAY SEVEN

I don't know where I am and no longer care how far I have hiked.
The rain finally stopped. Now I knew why the forests in Minnesota are so lush and green even though it was supposedly in a drought. Why my six days of hiking had been like taking a trip into the Amazon jungle. When it rains there, it can really, really rain. Too bad all this rain didn't come a few weeks earlier so there would have actually been water in the water sources on which I depended.

I was dry inside the tent, but outside everything was a muddy mess. Stuffing a muddy pile of clothing and gear into a backpack leads to an equally muddy pile of gear to set up in the next camp. I pleaded for bright sunshine and gentle breezes to dry everything out faster than you can say snot. Snot…Snot…Nope. That didn't work. Then I decided that perhaps the solution was to relax in my tent for a while and just let things dry. Hey, I figured, I'm on the relaxed plan now. I've wimped out—I mean, made the rational decision to end my trip sooner. I only had to hike a measly seven miles today. While justifying my lack of action in my tent, I heard a new noise. Yesterday afternoon's soft tinkle of Indian Camp Creek now sounded like a raging torrent. Like a real, swiftly moving stream, instead of something created by a giant taking a whiz.

Finally, I decided to face the medicine, emerge from my cocoon, and confirm my earlier diagnosis of how hard it rained: my plastic mug, which was about four inches tall, was filled to the brim with water. I scampered around, shaking off wet plastic bags, and pranced around camp en pointe trying not to get splashed. On the bright side, the rain had stopped, and I would soon be heading for a lake, which looked gorgeous on a map, not only because it was a big, blue body of water, but also because it meant there would actually be space to look at that was not covered with plants.

When it came time to get some water, I discovered that my little Indian Camp Creek looked like one of those fountains providing a liquid chocolate concoction at a fancy buffet. I stood there for a few moments, watching the gravy roar by, and confirmed that my decision to wimp out on this trip was a good one. But I was still thirsty and needed to find a way to get water from this brown effluent. I scooted up and down the creek and eventually found a slower-moving section and filtered away. The water that emerged into my bottle seemed to look OK, but my guess was that it would probably add to the misery going on in my belly.

Eventually, I couldn't wait any longer for my gear to dry, and I stuffed my soggy stuff in the pack and climbed steeply to the ridgeline. The trail wandered along the ridgetop, providing expansive views of the sea of green leaves that is the Minnesota forest, with just the thin, white stick trunks of the birch and aspen to contrast with all that green.

After lunch, I climbed to a view of Caribou Lake. It was an expansive body of water with a few cabins tucked along the shore. You heard that right. A freakin' lake. Other than the ocean-sized monster that is Superior, this is the first lake I'd seen in this purported Land of 10,000 Lakes. The good stuff was just beginning as I descended another mile to the lovely shores of Lake Agnes.

■   ■   ■

To this jaded guy who had spent his life hiking in the Sierra Nevada, this was what camping is all about. A luscious body of sparkling moisture surrounded by thick forest. My campsite sat on a tiny knoll just between the two nodes of the kidney-shaped lake. A gentle breeze sprung ripples that shimmered in the sunlight. I skipped around the campsite happily working away like Snow White. Hopefully, my singing was still a tenor and hadn't moved into the breaking-glass soprano that the Disney Snow White puts out. It's no wonder those seven little men work all day in dark caves instead of hanging out in the sunshine with the enchanting Miss Snow. That singing would make anyone want to head underground.

I hung up all the damp stuff to dry in the sunny breeze, stopping frequently to ponder the joy of an actual real-life lake right in my midst. I lazed out on the perfectly smooth, flat piece of rock touching the shore that had been in my dreams for the last week, and of course I had to go for a swim. It was a bit unnerving not being able to see the bottom while swimming around in what was the color of molasses, but it was not too cold and not too warm, with just the right amount of refreshment. I was reminded once again what I have always known. Sure, camp next to some teensy creek because you need the water or by a beaver pond because you are really desperate and there is absolutely no other alternative. But the best camping is always found along the shore of a lake.

Lakes are magnets. Suddenly, in a land of no people, they are here, because the water is here. On the opposite shore, I watched a family throwing rocks into the water, followed by a group of campers who walked by, mouths agape with desire, looking fondly at my campsite. Once they discovered that I had gotten there first, they moseyed on down the trail to find another spot, chiding each other that if they had only got out of bed sooner, they would have garnered the choice spot. While I have been a pinin' and a whinin' about the lack of people in the hood for days, now that they are here, of course I want them to stay a little farther away.

DAY EIGHT

The last day. Hallelujah. Still no longer caring how far I've hiked.

I woke up to wispy clouds dressed in bright purple and pink lace reflecting on the still surface of the lake. Millions of water bugs skated along the mirror, making raindrop-like ripples in the water. I turned in the other direction and found waves of misty fog slowly lifting above the dark-blue veneer of the lake. Billows of steam rolled across the water, then dissipated into the dark forest, as another wave of moisture slowly rose up from the water again. It was an incredible moment of pure bliss that can only come from quietly rolling out of your tent to a spectacular wilderness sunrise.

On the other hand, my stomach was getting worse—a constant barrage of gurgling and cramping. But I attempted to blot out that distraction and focus on the hard-fought (or perhaps hard-learned) lesson of this trip: quit focusing on the goal of hiking 235 miles, and instead savor what is going on in front of my eyes right now. When I think back on this trip, the shit that happened will certainly pop up, but it is that sunrise on the shore of Lake Agnes that will always be the indeleble memory of the trip.

■   ■   ■

Does this experience mean that I have to dial back my ambition a bit, only doing hikes where I will encounter more lakes instead of just more miles? Or perhaps it means I have to stop being so stubborn and bring a friend along so I can be slightly less batty? Life is short, and we need to focus on finding more Lake Agnes moments of bliss and fewer hot, five-mile slog fests that bring you to dusty, dried-up, disease-infested former beaver ponds. Duh.

OK, I do remember that no matter what you do, life does dish up its share of dried-up beaver ponds, but it would be nice to attempt to reduce the number of them. It's time I told myself the truth. I have met lots of people on the trail who can hike twenty-mile days by themselves day after day after day. Folks who seem to laugh in the face of cliff edges, blisters the size of grapes, and several mosquitoes in their ears and eyes at once as they chew up the miles. I have always really wanted to be that long-distance hiker. That guy who causes everybody to shake their head incredulously, either impressed with his capability or daunted that he would make such an effort. But guess what, Buckwheat? You ain't him. And I was finally realizing I never will be.

I'm more like all those other folks who love to get out in the woods for a few days or a week with some friends. It's more about the place I go than the number of miles I hike. The joy comes from moments, spent well. One right after another. A moment on the edge of a lake watching the sun slowly set, then another, watching it rise again the next morning at a place like Lake Agnes. Moments of stillness with the only sounds being a bird singing for a mate, or the wind rustling the leaves of a tree. And finally, on this special day, moments of bright sunshine, which dried my wet gear and got me on the trail for my last six miles of the trip. Just six little miles.

* * *

Well now, I do have to admit that in addition to the desire to quit hiking all day through jungle or dodging raging thunderstorms, I had another ulterior motive to escape from the Superior Hiking Trail near Lake Agnes. My cousin Cindi, who once again arrived to rescue me from my folly, had given me the choice when I called: join them on a trip to their cabin on tiny Saint Marys Island on Vermilion Lake in northern Minnesota, or continue hiking for three more days until she had returned from the cabin to pick me up. That was a no-brainer. I went for the island. I've always had a special place in my heart for islands. They are like castles with moats around them, providing a place of refuge from the marauders of the world. You can't just walk or drive to a little island on a lake, you need to make the commitment to get there by boat, and once you are there, there is nowhere to go but explore the borders of your little kingdom.

My parents spent twenty summers on one of the Muskoka Lakes north of Toronto. It's a wonderful *On Golden Pond* sort of place, which I was lucky enough to visit a number of times. Muskoka is sparkling, blue water dotted with wooden boats parrying past teeny granite islands covered with birch trees and sporting fascinating cabins leaning precariously over the water. My dad had spent his childhood summers in Muskoka living on Woodmere Island with his sister and seven brothers plying the water in wooden boats or cruising the lake for chicks, or whatever women were called back in the 1930s. Whenever I visited, the islands always enchanted me. We would stop off on Blueberry Island's granite wonderland for a picnic surrounded by water or visit the old Woodmere homestead, even though it had long since passed out of family hands.

About the time I did this hike, my parents realized they could no longer handle the rigors of the journey to Muskoka and had to sell their summer home. That summer, my dad still ably guided his precious wood boat around Lake Joseph, rumbling past the same rustic cottages hidden in the trees on windswept islands that he had been passing for seventy years. Etched upon his face was both deep appreciation for his long love affair with this place and melancholy that it was coming to an end.

Tiny Saint Marys Island is like a rustic version of Muskoka. A few small cabins, cool breezes, and lazy afternoons on the dock with a few breaks for a swim. I loved it. While Saint Marys was a true bromide after the trials of the trail, my stomach continued to gurgle and sent out regular zaps of pain like several small animals were digging their claws into my intestines. On the second day on the island, I noticed a stack of five-gallon jugs filled with water atop the refrigerator. When I asked Cindi about them, she said that was the drinking water and that she hoped I wasn't drinking the water from the lodge because it was unfiltered right out of the lake and not fit to be consumed. Gulp…or I wish I could have said, UnGulp. I hoped that the parasites I was getting from drinking the water from this lake would devour the parasites that I had apparently gotten from all those godforsaken beaver ponds.

6

Finding Peace at Fontanillis

AFTER THAT FIASCO IN MINNESOTA, I took a break from solo backpacking for a few years to thru-hike the Tahoe Rim Trail again in 2009 and 2011, this time as one of the leaders of the Tahoe Rim Trail Association's annual thru-hike. On these hikes, trail angels met us at road crossings every few days and brought utter joy, also known as pizza, ice cream, cold drinks, and warm smiles. Being with a group, however, was something I was still ambivalent about. Having someone to talk to on the trail certainly did help with the pangs of loneliness and would give my mind a break from the body aches, but it didn't take too long for all that blabbering to make me long for the meditation of silence I feel hiking alone.

For a number of years, I had been taking short backpacking trips with my daughters. If you enjoy being in the wilderness and are looking for something wonderful to do with your kids, this is the way to go. Don't plan on stacking up the miles, however, and be sure to bring a hefty supply of patience. Kids prefer hiking at glacial speed and are easily distracted by anything that will allow them to stop walking. One of my daughter's ploys was to tie her shoes poorly, so she had an excuse to come to a halt and tie them again.

A parent's job is to cajole, prod, threaten, and bribe their children to hike faster. I've tried Skittles, vivid descriptions of how gorgeous the destination was, and the always popular, "Hey, you know what the momma tomato says to the baby tomato (then with a slap of the hands together)...Ketch up!" It doesn't matter: everything you try will fail and will merely become an opportunity to vent your frustration. They will still continue at their snail's pace while dishing out a dose of nasty stink eye toward you for being so lame as to be occupying space. Eventually, hopefully before dark, you do reach the camping spot, where everything gets much better.

We would always spend two nights in the same place. A poorly executed layover day would eventually end my father-daughter backpacking trips, but before that, they were awesome. Where else in life do we get the opportunity to have absolutely no responsibilities for a whole day? You don't have to pack up your bag every morning and put another fifteen miles under your belt to reach the next stop on the map. Instead, you leisurely explore the world nearby. Surely, the most important benefit of these trips was that I was given the opportunity to spend some quality time with my daughters, who were both much more skilled than me at doing nothing. And doing nothing when you are with your children is actually doing something truly special.

One trip with Sarah brought us to American Lake, just below Lake Aloha's dam. It was a stunning little piece of granite amazingness, and for the most part we had it to ourselves. As they had done a number of times before, Sarah's friend Morgan and her dad, Dave, joined us. We were relaxed hiking companions and pretty comfortable with the whole doing-as-little-as-possible-on-the-layover-day thing.

On the second day, we dipped our bodies into the cool, refreshing water over and over, each time followed by flopping down onto the warm granite to dry off and release every muscle in our bodies. By the middle of the afternoon, feeling totally tranquil, I found a flat, smooth piece of rock, lay down, and gazed at the sky. To one side, a gurgling stream flowed into the rippled lake. To the other, waves softly lapped against the rocky shoreline. Above, soft, puffy clouds slowly floated past with the sun giving just enough heat to warm away the goosebumps. As the gentle wind touched me with magic fingers and the subtle scent of pine, I shut my eyes and disappeared into a quiet place in my soul where I could feel the earth traveling through the sky. Soon I felt totally connected to the earth and the universe. I had reached a point where the earth and I were one. If I had to put a name to what I was feeling, I would say I had reached a brief moment of enlightenment. But if you try to put a name to it, it makes the bubble of enlightenment go poof, and disappear.

■ ■ ■

After my bubble of enlightenment, in 2010 I headed over Kearsarge Pass into the Southern Sierra for a five-day trip with my friends Jan and Jan. On that trip, Jan No. 1 and I, both confirmed acrophobics, took turns choosing which of the exposed, knife-edged passes we would get all hollow stomach and weak-kneed on. It seems to help us get through the fear if we take turns being the one down on the ground pleading for mercy.

Jan and I had been confronting our fear of heights together ever since we summited Mount Whitney years earlier. Then, Jan and I joined our friend Laurie at Trail Crest. I remember this challenging section of trail at 13,600 feet as thirty feet of trail that was just three feet wide, and dropped down thousands of feet of sheer rock on both sides, giving those of us who suffer from vertigo a serious case of the weebie jeebies. While Laurie was prepared to do cartwheels across the narrow passage with her eyes closed, Jan and I sat silently in the wind at the edge of the abyss. Our brains already slightly warped by the lack of oxygen, we looked dizzily at the enormous drop-offs on both sides of the narrow trail, then at each other fearfully, then returned our spinning gaze back to the trail. Finally, I offered to go back down with her because I couldn't fathom actually walking across the chasm. But then, I discovered my spine and scampered full tilt across the section never raising my eyes from my feet. Jan looked up, and I was gone. She then got Laurie to help her across. Women, they have this uncanny ability to always be there for each other. What is up with that?

The summer of 2012 seemed to fly by without a long, grand adventure. Unless you count my first Burning Man…but that is a whole other book. Then, suddenly it was Labor Day, and I looked up and said, "Holy Shit, what the hell happened to summer?" Fortunately, summer was in no mood to go anywhere. The weather remained pleasant, the lakes stayed warm, and only the crowds of tourists had gone home. So I planned a three-day trip to Fontanillis Lake.

DAY ONE

The sun freshly dipped behind the Dicks Peak ridge, but the far-off east shore of Lake Tahoe was still lit up bright in the sunshine. I lay on the glacier-smoothed granite, waiting patiently for the impending alpen-glow show. Just to my west sat a snippet of gray shimmer, Fontanillis Lake, with Dicks Peak's dark-red summit reaching loftily above. To the east, a bustling cascade rushed down smooth rock to heart-and-lung-shaped Upper Velma Lake, a patch of blue surrounded by rich-green forest. As opposed to the zoo-like atmosphere that it takes on midsummer, on a weekday evening in late September, Desolation

Wilderness was living up to its name. There was not a human soul to be seen or heard.

■ ■ ■

I wrote a piece a few years ago about a crazy Saturday evening in early August at Middle Velma Lake. I called it "Assholes in the Woods." Still haven't found a publisher. Perhaps magazines are too busy extolling the joys of wilderness to talk about the kerfuffle that occurs when we all end up there at once. At least one hundred people were besieging the poor lake the night I arrived. The lake was surely just hoping that all these damn humans would go back to work and school soon and take their toilet paper with them. One bright bulb was yelling across the lake telling the world about his plans for immediate inebriation: "I'm going to get shitfaced! Woo hoo!" Another was trying to locate his berry good friend three hundred yards away: "Huckleberry... Where are you? Huckleberry!" In other words, folks were generally not practicing Leave No Trace Recommendation No. 7, which says, "Be Considerate of Other Visitors."

In general, people head into the wilderness with one of two goals: One group goes there to find solitude and peace; they wish to quietly contemplate their existence while appreciating the simple joys of nature. For others, the goal is to get shitfaced while yelling and screaming really loudly, because that is something they don't get to do in their apartment in the city without the management calling the police. As you can imagine, these two options don't reconcile.

■ ■ ■

What I attempted to do on this short solo hike was to learn once again how to focus on what is going on around me. To appreciate this moment. Right now. After setting up camp, I strolled down to the shore. While gazing out at the rocky crags and few remaining patches of snow on the shoulder of Dicks Peak, I heard a plop. An especially large trout was swimming back and forth just a foot off shore. It came up frequently to nibble at the surface but didn't appear to have a care in the world, or at least it wasn't worried about me. "Hey, he ain't got no fishing pole," he was probably saying. In case you are wondering why fish talk like they are on *The Andy Griffith Show*, it's because they live in the country. I sat there peacefully for about a half hour, watching the fish bob back and forth around the shoreline, content to quietly witness nature.

DAY TWO

One of the joys of having a layover day is that you can venture off on a pleasant day hike with a lightweight pack. In just an hour and a half, I was atop Dicks Pass, a long haul for a day hiker coming in from Emerald Bay, or as noted in Chapter Four, a grueling afternoon on the Tahoe Rim Trail for the hiker carrying his whole life on his back on Day Twelve. Still feeling frisky at the top, I made my first venture along the ridgeline between Dicks Pass and Mount Tallac. It was a route I had never explored before, because usually by the time I got there I was too exhausted to take on any extra distance. It was a slow progression along the dark, volcanic rock-topped ridge, but the reward was my first glimpse of Kalmia Lake.

Kalmia on a map looks to be just a short distance from the Bayview Trail, which was the route I took to get to Fontanillis. From above I realized, however, that there was an incredibly steep slope of sheer rock and gravel between the lake's shore and me. From below, it appeared even more daunting: smooth cliffs interspersed with thick forest hanging on a precipitous slope. I will likely never reach Kalmia's shores, but from atop that ridge I could sit quietly and appreciate its beauty. I was trying very hard to teach myself that was enough.

I made my way back along the ridge to Dicks Pass. And with time on my hands and nowhere to be, I sat down to focus on what nature would reveal to me. If I am quiet, Mother Nature will let me feel her presence. I can't decide whether the term Mother Nature is appropriate. I used to think that the earth and mountains were male, and the lakes, meadows, and living things were feminine. But I am beginning to feel that the heart and soul of nature is feminine. Either way, she is there. Ready to be understood if we remain still and decide to let her into our hearts. Perhaps as we learn to understand nature, we can learn to better understand ourselves. Hiking with others gives us a chance to understand communication and relationships without the static of civilization. Hiking alone, we can reach into our hearts and touch our souls. The trick might be to really appreciate what we find when we touch it.

It can feel raw and scary to touch our soul. To understand the true essence of who we are, which we don't see in the midst of the daily grind of work, family, money, traffic, and Facebook. It is then that we might finally realize that we are alone, which might make us feel empty and lonely at first, but being alone doesn't have to mean lonely. It can also mean just being by yourself. Experiencing life on our terms. It's powerful to learn that all we need is inside us.

■ ■ ■

After returning to camp and setting myself up again on the massive granite rock which afforded views of Upper Velma Lake and in the distance a sliver of Lake Tahoe, I continued my meditative thought process and wrote this:

> Being alone in nature is meditation. Whether it is the rhythm of walking or dancing to the music of the wind and the birds. When we contemplate a fish leisurely waving its tail and sliding through water, a tree softly waving in the breeze, a rock absorbing heat from the sun, then releasing it into the night. When we learn to appreciate shape, contour, slope, we become one…but then…"Holy shit! I just got buzzed by a hawk!" Apparently, the hawk must have been floating very low, following the contour of the slope, then swooped just over the pile of rocks below my view spot, and had to rise hurriedly to avoid whopping me in the head. It missed me by an inch.

Shortly thereafter a yellow jacket buzzed around my ear, setting me off on a quick jig trying to get it to go away. And then there was that fly, you know the one that would not take "No!" for an answer as it buzzed over and over around my eyes.

It's times like this that remind us that nature is not always the quiet, relaxing meditation that we envision as a yogi sitting cross-legged on a mountain top with soft Enya music playing in the background. It's often messy, chaotic, and filled with pesky challenges. It's a rock reaching up to make you smash to the ground as you stroll along the trail with your brain in never-never land. It's losing your balance and slow-motion face-planting into the water while attempting to rock-dance your way across a bustling stream. And of course it is often attempting to refrain from going stark raving loony when a dozen flies are simultaneously dive-bombing your head. But these are just nature's way of testing our strength, willpower, and ability to move past distractions.

Perhaps we can never reach the goal that Eastern philosophy calls enlightenment, peace, or true self. But hiking alone can give us time and a freeness of mind to help us figure out that it might be at least a worthwhile goal. Being close to our hearts and facing our thoughts gives our brain the time and freedom to ask the right questions, even if we do not as yet know the answers. Or would know what to do about it if we did.

It's the beauty and simple complexity of nature that allows our brains to escape the mundane everydayness and look inward. We may not be as brave as we try to tell ourselves we are. But with the knowledge that we are actually chickens, we can begin the process of becoming brave. It is only in looking inward and discovering for ourselves our strengths and weaknesses that we become warriors. The support of others is helpful, but it's just a stopgap measure until we dig deep and find our own strength.

I was discovering that perhaps it was this leisurely three-day trip that would allow me to find the meditative benefits of a solo hike. The long hike gets you away from the world for an extended time, but being hell-bent to get somewhere, I became focused on the miles and the pain more than looking inward. On the leisurely trip, I can let the day lazily pass. A day perhaps that I have set aside, with the sole purpose just to observe, both inside and out. And if I don't like what I see inside, I shouldn't blame the solitude. Instead, I should use it as an impetus for change.

■   ■   ■

I crossed the creek by my campsite, looking for that big black hunk of granite that I saw last night with a fleeting thought it could be a bear… and then it occurred to me that I had reached a state of free play. I was just exploring, finding whatever interesting things nature sent my way, then following it wherever it led me. Like we all used to do when we were kids before it was scheduled, structured, and scared out of us.

Perhaps I relearned the ability to play on my trip to Burning Man, which is basically a humongous sandbox for adults. There you learn that when you leave your dusty camp, it is best not to set out to do anything in particular, but just to get on your bike and see where it leads you. It takes a few days, but you learn to follow your instinct, with the knowledge that wherever you end up is where you are meant to be. As long as you are open to discovering and, most importantly, joining in whatever you discover, you will find the true joy of play. And thus happiness. I was discovering that every day in the wilderness I should carry out my life like it was a day at Burning Man, except instead of whimsical art, the constant barrage of techno noise, and dodging drugged-out ravers, I would follow the subtle sounds and sights of nature. And be open to wherever it might take me.

DAY THREE

Just before dark on Day Two, I noticed a fellow traveler pumping water out of the lake then disappearing to his campsite on the other side of the creek. I never heard or saw him again until the morning, when while I was lazing in the sun on my flat piece of granite overlooking the lake, he appeared, seemingly from nowhere, just below me saying…"Are you the guy who wrote the book about the Tahoe Rim Trail?" He had run into a group of three I had seen heading up Dicks Pass the day before. One of the group was a lady I knew who was finishing up the Tahoe Rim Trail, and I passed along a few trail tips (like if you are going to get over Dicks Pass and out to Fallen Leaf Lake before dark, you better stop talking to me and get your ass in gear).

My new friend and I talked for a half hour about the Tahoe Rim Trail, hiking, and life. He thought he was gaining information from a guy who wrote a book about hiking, but I felt that I was the winner in the knowledge-gaining contest. Here's a guy who made the decision to backpack the day before he hit the trail and actually followed through and did it. He brought very little in the way of food and gear, but felt that he had all that he really needed. He didn't seem the least bit worried about whether he was missing anything. Listening to his attitude and perspective made me evaluate my own. I sometimes spend so much time planning and double-checking myself every step of the way that I miss the opportunity just to play.

When our conversation was complete, I headed home. I was in the right place. Doing what I was supposed to be doing. Walking and watching the world slowly roll by. Living in rhythm. Walking in meditation.

■ ■ ■

I lay naked on a flat piece of granite just at the edge of Middle Velma Lake after a quick and cold dip in her silent waters. I honored this sacred lake, apologizing for the abuse it receives every year from the hordes of visitors. Now, with the crowds dissipated, the lake finally has its chance to breathe. Nine months of peace before the three-month onslaught of toilet-paper flags and screaming revelers.

I lay there not thinking of the litany of positives and negatives that is a day in the wilderness alone. Just feeling the warmth of the sun, the smooth coolness of the rock, and the gentle scent of pine. I listened to the soft rustle of the grasses and the gentle lapping of water meeting rock. Enjoying doing absolutely nothing, alone in the world.

Epilogue

THIS MANUSCRIPT LANGUISHED in the deep recesses of my computer for six years while life flowed in new directions. Then in early 2020, I read several humorous books from Michael Branch about his life in the Nevada desert. They tell his tale about the importance of time spent wandering alone in the sagebrush near his home. I also made a return read of Edward Abbey and his solo adventures in Utah. This gave me a hankering to delve into the book again, but it was actually the pandemic lockdown of 2020 and all that stay-at-home time when I was looking for a positive outlet that got me to focus on completing this book in my backyard under the Jeffrey pines and white firs.

Since I first wrote of my solo journeys, my daughters have gone off to their new adventurous lives with careers and partners thousands of miles away, and I have discovered a new venture of my own. No longer married, for the past five years, I've been in a loving and lovely relationship with Joyce, who actually likes to hike. And backpack. With me even. Preposterous.

We haven't set out on lengthy thru-hikes. We instead focus on shorter distances with the primary goal to escape the crowds and spend nights under the stars. One of our favorite trips was for five days in the Southern Sierra, spending most of the time well above 10,000 feet. Three of those nights were in one camp, setting out on leisurely day hikes with light packs in search of wildflowers, ancient trees, luscious meadows, and solitude.

On the second day, we climbed to a high-altitude piece of paradisal wonderland. A cascade drops through a field of talus from a sheer granite slope to a meadow. It carries gray glacial till as it meanders through a small patch of luscious grass before swiftly dropping through more talus to the forest below. The meadow was a wave of bright-orange paintbrush, tiger lilies, and iris, with soft grass along the creek's edge that looked like a mown green on a golf course. It was a luscious refuge of boisterous life, surrounded by stark, lifeless crags sporting patches of snow. We feel we would be dishonoring the private joy it gave us by disclosing its name, but for us, just a mention of the place will move our lips and eyes to smile.

We revel in layover days. The camp is set; there are not many miles to go before we sleep. There is little to be done, so we become children exploring our surroundings. Watching for what nature provides: An osprey plunging her talons into the water to scoop up a trout. One of the lucky trout who escaped the osprey gently twisting along the shoreline. A pine marten furtively wandering through our camp. And the world's best twice-a-day picture show: the slow ascent of the sun in the morning and its slow descent in the evening. Followed in the stark quiet of wilderness night, with the endless universe of stars and galaxies over our heads.

When it came time for me to update the Tahoe Rim Trail guidebook, Joyce used it as an excuse to hike with me as I reacquainted myself with the trail. In so doing, she completed the TRT herself. It's been thirteen years since my first circumnavigation of the Tahoe Rim Trail. What I noticed the most this time around was that so many more people were on the trail. During my first trip, I had Marlette Peak Campground to myself in the middle of summer. When Joyce and I arrived there in the middle of the week in September, the dusty campground was full to the gills with thru-hikers. A truly solo hiking experience is no longer an easy thing to achieve.

Now when I arrive at camp, I'm still tired as always. But it is a joy to have someone with whom to share the experience and burdens. A sounding board for my ideas. Emotional support to get through the darkness. Sure, hiking with someone else is a compromise. There are many times when I'm standing, tapping my feet for what seems like forever, wondering what in the hell is taking her so long. And that's just in the parking lot while she is organizing her pack. I'm sure that she is looking at me many times and wondering: "When is he going to stop talking?"

■   ■   ■

When we climbed up the brutally steep ascent to Baker Lake in the backwaters of Great Basin National Park, I spent most of the time hiking solo. Every few minutes, I would stop to count to ten and see if she was still in sight range and continue on. When I stopped to catch my breath, she would catch up and then give me an exasperated look when I turned around and started tromping up the hill again. She has taught me that it's OK to hike with a partner and not talk to them for mile after mile. I'd always thought that dead air between humans was not polite. But now I've learned that it's a good thing to just roll along the trail, enjoy the quiet, and ponder what goes in and out of my brain. Which if things are going well is not much. Just the sound of breath and crunching feet, and the feel of the air against my skin.

■   ■   ■

Once we finally made it to the lake, we found an idyllic, little grove of mountain hemlock pines to hide our tent and a luxurious, smooth, flat, grassy area with perfectly placed rocks for back rests. We spent much of the next three days leaning against those rocks, reading books, writing in journals, and taking frequent breaks to silently gaze at the mountains. We enjoy the solitude together. Maybe we have discovered that you can hike together and still enjoy some of the benefits of hiking alone. Perhaps that is what I've been searching for all along.

Works Cited

"Fear of Rest" by Wayne Muller, published in *Sabbath: Restoring the Sacred Rhythm of Rest* (New York: Bantam Books, 1999).

"What is Solitude?" by Hara Estroff Marano, published in *Psychology Today,* July 1, 2003.

The Eight Wilderness Discovery Books by John Muir (Seattle: The Mountaineers Books, 1992).

Tahoe Sierra: A Natural History Guide to 112 Hikes in the Northern Sierra by Jeffrey P. Schaffer (Berkeley, CA: Wilderness Press, 1998).

Yosemite Nature Notes, Volume xv, Number 5, May 1936.

John Charles Frémont journals, as quoted in *American History* by Graeme Mercer Adam and Charles Wentworth Upham (New York: The University Society, 1905).

Blue Highways: A Journey into America by William Least Heat-Moon (Boston: Little, Brown Books, 1982).

Thru Hiker's Guide to America: 25 Incredible Trails You Can Hike in One to Eight Weeks by E. Schlimmer (Camden, ME: Ragged Mountain Press, 2005).

About the Author

TIM HAUSERMAN is a freelance writer and longtime resident of Lake Tahoe. He has written hundreds of articles for a variety of publications on travel, outdoor recreation, housing, education, wildfire, and other issues. He wrote *Monsters in the Woods: Backpacking with Children,* published by the University of Nevada Press. He also wrote *Tahoe Rim Trail: The Official Guide for Hikers, Mountain Bikers, and Equestrians; Cross-Country Skiing in the Sierra: The Best Resorts and Touring Centers in California and Nevada;* and a children's book, *Gertrude's Tahoe Adventures in Time.*